THE MASTER ARCHITECT SERIES II

Norman Foster

Selected and Current Works of

Foster and Partners

Norman Foster

Selected and Current Works of
Foster and Partners

First published in Australia in 1997 by
The Images Publishing Group Pty Ltd
ACN 059 734 431
6 Bastow Place, Mulgrave, Victoria, 3170
Telephone (61 3) 9561 5544 Facsimile (61 3) 9561 4860

National Library of Australia Cataloguing-in-Publication Data

    Foster and Partners.
       Norman Foster: selected and current works of Foster and Partners

       Bibliography.
       Includes index.
       ISBN 1 875498 57 5
       Master Architect Series II ISSN 1320 7253

       1. Foster, Norman. 2. Architecture, Modern—20th
       century—Great Britain. 3. Architecture, British.
       4. Architects—Great Britain. I. Title.
       (Series: Master architect series 2).

   720.92

Edited by Stephen Dobney
Designed by The Graphic Image Studio Pty Ltd,
Mulgrave, Australia
Film by Scanagraphix Australia Pty Ltd
Printing by Everbest Printing, Hong Kong

Contents

Contents Continued

Profile

INTRODUCTION

Introduction

By Sir Norman Foster

This publication coincides with the celebration of more than 30 years of practice in architecture and design. My colleagues and I, under one title or another, have worked together on several hundred projects since the mid-1960s. The selection of buildings and projects illustrated in this book reflects the type, range and scale of work undertaken over this period. More significantly, the process of reviewing these projects has caused me to reflect upon the consistency of approach that underpins this diverse and varied body of work. The benefit of hindsight, and a degree of post-rationalisation, allow me to trace a pattern of thinking, an attitude to the process of design, that weaves its way through many of our projects. One part of this can be defined as an interest in the invention and re-invention of the building type. Another part relates to integration. For me, the optimum design solutions integrate social, technological, aesthetic or economic needs which are often in conflict.

At a personal level, I confess to being obsessed with invention. Part of this obsession is a fascination with inquiry—with "going back to basics". I have to understand the underlying principles of a problem in order to question the traditional response and identify if there is an opportunity to invent or re-invent a solution. Together with my colleagues, I design buildings in the hope that they take forward the boundaries of knowledge and experience of each particular building type.

Airports—a new typology

When we were confronted with the challenge to design London's third airport at Stansted, the client defined the needs for a new generation airport: a structure that would cost less to build and run, would work better than previous airports and would also offer greater security. While nobody could dispute the importance of these goals, for me the new generation airport also had a very strong social imperative. Ideally it should help to turn the experience of air travel from one of misery to one of delight—to try to rediscover the friendliness, orientation and sense of occasion that had typified great terminals of the past, particularly in the railway age.

The conventional solution to the airport building type which has developed since World War 2 is a box with a highly serviced roof structure which contains or supports large amounts of machinery and equipment. The effect of this top-heavy solution, full of ductwork, pipes and electric lighting, has been dark and congested environments which are hostile to the users as well as being difficult to service and maintain without disrupting passenger movements. The resulting concourses are almost black boxes and create a spiral of energy consumption. Artificial lighting adds to the heat load from people and increases the demand for cooling which consumes yet more energy. This in turn requires more equipment and a more expensive structure to support it.

At Stansted we questioned the appropriateness of this "conventional wisdom" and, after much research and analysis, ended up literally turning the problem on its head. All of those services normally housed on the roof are far better placed in an undercroft below concourse level where they are out of sight and easier to maintain. The lower level also accommodates the baggage handling systems, creating a logical separation of baggage at ground level and passengers above—exactly where each needs to be to connect with the aircraft that serve them.

The undercroft is a large-scale equivalent of the floor void in a modern office building. In both cases the objective is to provide flexibility for change over time. In the case of an office, it might allow changes in the wiring or the introduction of new fibre optic information technology. At the scale of Stansted it allowed a main-line railway station to be inserted when the building was already under construction. The undercroft also provides easy access to the air-conditioning plant, chillers, lighting, and other equipment that requires regular servicing and more frequently needs to be replaced.

The concept of servicing the spaces from below offers wonderful spatial benefits. The clutter of pipes, ductwork and light fittings—as well as the problems of suspended ceilings—are gone. Instead there is the formal clarity of structure and the joy of natural light. The roof is in effect a lighting screen which also offers protection from the elements. Its appearance is deceptively simple and belies the many hours of creative struggle to model and develop the final concept.

Although the levels of natural light are high and have resulted in dramatic energy savings, the glazed roof openings occupy a mere 5 per cent of the total area. Solar gain is reduced by the perforated metal panels suspended below the openings. As well as being sculptures in space, these kite-like panels also perform other important functions. By reflecting natural light back onto the surrounding surfaces of the structural vaults, they visually lighten the entire roof, enhancing its floating appearance. At night they mask the "black hole" effect of the roof openings above them and, when artificially lit from the base of the structural trees, they help to reflect light back into the space. Significantly, they are also designed to allow controlled shafts of sunlight to penetrate, bringing the floors to life with patterns of light and shade.

The undercroft also had other environmental benefits. It enabled the building to be partially buried into the gentle slope of the site so that on the land side it would fit discreetly into the rural landscape, comfortably below the existing treeline. This was not only socially desirable, but it was also a political necessity. The location of London's third airport had been subject to many years of indecision and policy changes; over time, the issue of environmental impact had grown in importance so that it was critical to develop a design which was sensitive to these concerns.

Only by questioning the basic principles of an airport did we succeed in coming up with a solution that works more efficiently than the traditional model, as well as having clear spatial and economic benefits. The inverted building type is a re-invention of the airport typology. This strategy has informed a number of other airport projects developed by our studio for Bangkok and Shanghai and has been further refined at Chek Lap Kok Airport in Hong Kong. While Chek Lap Kok stretches the limits of the building type—in terms of scale, legibility, construction and implementation—it is Stansted's radical spatial and tectonic structure which has pushed forward the boundaries in the field and has been widely adopted by other designers and client organisations, leading to a new generation of airport terminals around the world.

Workplace—the social imperative

A similar quest for innovation has generated radical solutions for the workplace, from factories to offices and corporate headquarters.

As early as 1966 our project for Reliance Controls broke the mould of traditional factory buildings in the quest to improve working standards in the new electronics industries. It did this by questioning the segregated model of "management box and workers' shed" with its implications of "we and they", "posh and scruffy", "front and back", "clean and dirty". Instead, a democratic pavilion was proposed with a single entrance, uniform standards throughout and flexible open space which could be changed over time, according to the varying demands of production and administration.

This process of "back-to-basics" questioning was central to the design concept of the Willis Faber & Dumas headquarters developed in the early 1970s when most offices were compartmentalised into individual cells or large shopfloor spaces. Discussions with future users identified the desirability of collective space—something that could re-establish a sense of community within a growing company. Our response was to turn the entire circulation system of the building into a single social space by drawing the main escalators through an inclined atrium with natural top light, situated in the heart of the building. I can remember the company secretary, Ken Knight, standing in this space and explaining how it worked to groups of visitors. He would describe how I had rejected the idea of lifts in the new building on the grounds that they were antisocial, and how I had proposed escalators instead. He then went on to explain that in their previous offices everyone would avoid eye contact in the lifts, but here in Ipswich it was a different story. Everyone greeted each other in the morning as they rode the escalators and exchanged pleasantries during the day. For him it brought back the spirit of the family firm in the days when it was much smaller, and re-established the identity of the company.

While I am delighted that the building is today celebrated for its formal and aesthetic attributes (like nearby Ely Cathedral, it was recently protected by a Grade I listing), I still find its social and technical diagram the most compelling and rewarding aspect of this milestone project.

The headquarters building for the Hongkong and Shanghai Banking Corporation takes some of these themes further, for example, almost all the floors are connected by escalators, which is unique in a high-rise building. But more importantly, the desire for a powerful public symbol and flexible business space led to the invention of a new form of spatial organisation. Before this building, every skyscraper had a central core which accommodated services and vertical circulation. The design for the Hongkong and Shanghai Bank broke this tradition by fragmenting the core and dispersing it to two of the four edges.

This plan creates better office spaces with views in two directions and an unbroken line of sight from one side to the other. Another benefit is that, unlike the single extrusion of a central core building, the bank's profile on the skyline can change, creating deep spaces at the base and slimmer spaces at the top. Vertically, the scale of the building is broken down by double-height reception areas served by high-speed lifts. The result is a series of village-like clusters, one above the other, rather than the anonymity of a traditional office tower.

Without the interruption of a solid core, the spaces are also far more adaptable to change. This flexibility has been put to the test by the many departmental changes which have occurred since the building first opened. In the past, these would have involved considerable upheaval while building work was carried out: instead, they have been achieved by the bank's own staff during a weekend operation. More recently, the bank has been able to incorporate a large dealers' floor into their tower, something which none of their competitors has been able to achieve in a high-rise headquarters building.

Another key generator of the bank's design is its relationship to the public realm and the city. The building is lifted off the ground, creating a generous, protected civic space at the crossroads of central Hong Kong. The original notion that this large institution should "give something back" to the city has become a tangible reality over the last few years. During the working week the space acts as a formal meeting place and a glass showcase to the process of banking.

At weekends it is transformed into an informal gathering place and a favourite spot for impromptu picnics. It is the multiplicity of social, commercial and urban activities, as well as the radical core plan, that constitutes its re-invention of the office high-rise.

Cities—the interplay of micro and macro scales

At the global level, the late 20th century is witnessing an exponential growth in urbanisation. In the West we are faced with the inevitable decline of the inner city, brought about by the demise of the manufacturing industries and increased social deprivation. At the macro scale, the environmental impact of cities—their effect on global energy consumption and pollution—is now firmly placed on the international political agenda. The health of our cities is seen as critical to global welfare.

Yet, at the micro scale, the design of the very spaces that bring people together—the public realm—is often ignored. As designers we have a social and political responsibility to nurture the public realm. It is this approach—mediation between the macro and the micro scales—that has informed the design strategy of a number of recent urban projects that we have undertaken in Nîmes, Duisburg, Rotterdam and London. In all these projects the process of "invention" has gravitated around the notion of the public realm.

The current World Squares project in London is representative of this approach. Together with colleagues from associated design disciplines, we are responsible for upgrading and reconfiguring a central slice of the historic city. The site includes some of the capital's most familiar urban landmarks—Trafalgar Square, Parliament Square and Whitehall. This is the London of picture postcards, the home of the Palace of Westminster, Westminster Abbey and the National Gallery. As the heart of the nation's institutions of government, monarchy and culture, the area is visited by nearly 20 million tourists a year. Yet, sadly, the urban setting of these historic monuments has become badly degraded. The streets have been ravaged by asphalt and the motor car, with a consequent erosion of the public realm that mars the everyday urban experience.

As part of our research on the project, we examined the structure of this area of the city and its relationship to greater London—an analysis of the parts and the whole. We also undertook a detailed traffic study of vehicles and pedestrians. Using the techniques developed by the Space Syntax Laboratory, we tracked pedestrian movements and analysed patterns of behaviour of tourists and local people. We looked at where people sat to eat their sandwiches and how they crossed the perilous roads to get views of the surrounding monuments. We looked for the deep structure of the city at many levels.

Only then did I feel ready to put forward a design proposal for this key area in central London, a design which clearly builds upon the rich historic fabric of buildings and public spaces, synthesising the old and the new. The urban diagram for World Squares is founded on a few simple gestures that give priority to public space. The pedestrian "body" of major spaces—Trafalgar Square, Parliament Square and Old Palace Yard—is widened and made more accessible. New gathering points are provided that take into account vistas and through movements in the area. Some key roads, but not all, are closed to through traffic. Attention is given to new surfaces and urban furniture that reclaim the public realm for the visitor and Londoner alike.

In Berlin, where we are reconstructing the Reichstag as the new seat of government for Germany, we have preserved the history of this monument by revealing memories of its past. Remnants of the

19th century masonry are exposed alongside graffiti from the Russian occupation, as well as the imprints of the 1950s. However, there is a clear distinction between these fragments of the past and the most recent intervention—our major transformation that will create a new Bundestag for the 21st century. In this, and other projects like it, the richness and variety of each period is enhanced by the layers of time. At the macro scale it is the contributions of different ages that makes a city more vibrant and richer; at the micro scale this is also true of the fabrics of those historic structures which are in search of a new lease of life.

Mindful of the wider issues of energy consumption, pollution and global warming, our design for the Reichstag also has a significant environmental dimension. The new German Parliament will be the first major public building in the world to be powered and climate-controlled entirely by renewable sources of energy. Oil from vegetable sources—rape or sunflower seed oil—will be burnt in a cogenerator to produce electricity. The process is clean, with a minimal discharge of atmospheric pollution. Waste, in the form of heat, is converted into cooling by feeding it into a heat absorption unit. Heated or chilled water is transported to thin radiators embedded in the ceilings, walls or floor surfaces to heat or cool the spaces. There are none of the traditional big ducts transporting large volumes of air—no grilles or suspended ceilings.

Further refinements in the Reichstag project include deep bore holes which can collect excess heat produced in the summer and store it in underground lakes for recovery during the following winter as a thermal energy source. Arrays of photovoltaic cells on the south-facing roof slopes also contribute electrical energy. The total system is sufficiently compact and efficient to serve the demands of the entire quarter in which the Reichstag is located; it is, in effect, a mini ecological power station.

The nature of design

Words cannot describe the appearance, feel or workings of a building—the experience of spaces, inside or outside, deserted or inhabited, involves all of our senses. When I try to explain any project with words, it becomes apparent, as I weave from the social to the technical to the aesthetic, from one concern to another, that the design is about merging or integrating the many worlds of separate disciplines.

It is not possible to separate the nature of design from the process that conceives it. If the built reality is the embodiment of diverse disciplines, then it should surely follow that the conception of the design must harness the talents of individuals with those specialist skills.

This does not mean that I am advocating a "design by committee" approach—nothing could be further from the truth. As an architect I regard it as an essential part of my mission to attempt to inspire a network of independence which transcends contractual obligations, to search for an order with shared human values. The right chemistry of human relationships is essential in this process because it entails individuals from widely differing backgrounds sharing and interacting together. Strong leadership is needed and this may pass from one group to another over the long time-span of a project. Continuity of the same set of values that inspired the project is also critical.

In many significant projects the integration of the political initiative is as essential as the philosophical component. To illustrate the relationship between the worlds of politics, philosophy and innovation I have selected two projects which do not belong to the traditional category of buildings normally associated with architecture, but are closer to the category of infrastructure or engineering. Such projects are often more significant in their impact on our environment than an individual building. Both of the schemes I have chosen are influenced by the political integration of Europe, which has stimulated the construction of new transportation and communication networks. Some, like roads and bridges, are highly visible; others pass invisibly via satellites in outer space, but even they need prominent earth-based towers or platforms.

In the first category is the bridge over the Tarn Valley at Millau in the Massif Central which will eventually connect France and Spain by high-speed auto routes. The project is heroic in scale and dimensions. Horizontally, it is 2.5 kilometres long and so high above the deepest part of the valley that the Eiffel Tower could easily be inserted below it with room to spare.

Not surprisingly, each of the teams which competed for this project was dominated by engineers but all were set up from the outset with an architect presence. At the time of the final jury I was persuaded by my engineer colleagues to explain the philosophy behind the concept. In the discussion period that followed, the engineers were to have full opportunity to explain the technicalities of the proposal.

Many of the teams had started from the proposition that the river, after which the valley had been named, demanded a large-span structure, perhaps a symbolic arch. I demonstrated with photos and sketches that the river was quite insignificant in the landscape: whether travelling by plane or car or on foot, you were hardly aware of it. The bridge was not about spanning the river at all. The true challenge was to span from one plateau to another, 2.5 kilometres across the valley; to create a road in the sky with the most minimal physical intervention—supports that would march across the terrain at the most economically wide span. This led us to design a cable-stayed structure that was a taut and delicate balance between the world of nature and the man-made. The logic and aesthetic of the structure followed from a philosophical stance about the very essence of the task, and it was the philosophy which separated our project from the others.

In Barcelona it was the political philosophy of a visionary mayor that was to provide the catalyst for a new form of communications structure. The city was overlooked by the mountains of Collserola, already blighted by unsightly masts and satellite dishes. In the run-up to the 1992 Olympics, plans had been announced by two television companies and the telephone monopoly to each build their own tall tower on the mountains. The response of the mayor was to say that Collserola was a protected site—a national park—and that the vistas out from the city were too important to be compromised by a forest of towers. Instead, he decreed that there would be one tower only, to be used by everyone.

Within this context we were able to design a single structure—a series of gravity-defying "tables-in-the-sky". The tower has become a powerful symbol of Barcelona's regeneration. Apart from its contribution to the urban skyline, the tower and its viewing platform have become a much-used facility by visitors to the Collserola park. It is a synthesis of innovation in architecture, engineering and politics, and its strength is rooted in the integration of political decision-making and the process of design.

Looking at the projects I have selected to explore the themes of invention and integration, I am conscious of the way in which the schemes relate to one another, even though they are all specific to their place and totally different in appearance. Despite the fact that design is not a linear sequence, there does seem to be a pattern.

Points of creative departure often seem to be followed by periods of reflection and consolidation. Yet the same pattern is evident during those bleak periods when there were few opportunities to build—the energy would be absorbed into hypothetical projects and competitions only to surface later when the right commission would arise.

Although an individual project might be a search for an inner order—a marriage of the functional and spiritual—there is at times a randomness which informs the development of one scheme relative to another. At work in the studio, I am often surrounded by sketches, drawings and models of ongoing projects. I look at them from distant and oblique views—quite distinct from formal design reviews. As a backdrop to my daily existence they come into focus at the least expected moments. Perhaps in the middle of a phone call I can see something in a different way. I make connections and associations—sometimes visual, sometimes literary—with other projects and artefacts.

As the illustrations in this book confirm, this process has resulted in a variety of built forms and solutions. Each building is different, charged with a different symbolic and aesthetic value that transcends the resolution of its functional programme. But the body of work as a whole constitutes a "collective memory" which provides a springboard for the next generation of designs and inventions.

I sometimes visualise our work as a series of beads on a string, each bead representing a project along the timeline. Some beads loom larger than others—these are the ones that, in my view, have moved the boundaries of invention forward. Others have further developed or consolidated important concepts. But each of them contributes, in its own way, to the collective search for clarity—a search that drives my passion for design.

Adapted from a longer essay by Sir Norman Foster.

SELECTED WORKS

Creek Vean House

Design/Completion 1964/1966
Cornwall, England
Mr and Mrs Marcus Brumwell
350 square metres
Concrete block load-bearing walls, in-situ concrete floors
Blockwork, glass, slate and turfed roof

This private house, built on a steeply sloping site, has been designed to exploit classic Cornish views of wooded valleys, a creek with bobbing boats and, to the south, the broad sweep of the Fal estuary.

Early designs retained an existing bungalow and envisaged a cascading glass roof and continuous buttress walls descending to the boathouse below. The final design of the house—more complex, less uncompromising and more picturesque—organises the composition around two routes: one external, the other internal. The external route bridges a dry moat between the lane and the house and runs past the front door and down a flight of steps to the waterfront. The internal route takes the form of a toplit picture gallery following the contour line and linking all the living spaces into a single continuum.

Continued

1

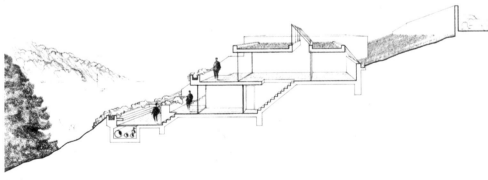

2

1 Concept sketch by Norman Foster
2 Early design: sectional perspective
3 View from creek
4 Steps from creek to house
5 View of gallery corridor
6 Double-height living space
7 Planted roof

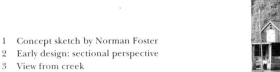

3

4

20

Materials—honey-coloured concrete blocks with blue Welsh slate floors—have been left to speak for themselves. The design of the double-height glazed wall of the two-storey living and dining area, composed of frameless sliding sashes carried in front of a mezzanine, foreshadows many later Foster buildings.

5

6

7

IBM Pilot Head Office

Design/Completion 1970/1971
Cosham, Hampshire, England
IBM (UK) Ltd
8,400 square metres
Steel columns and lattice trusses on ground-bearing in-situ concrete slab
Steel, solar glazing, neoprene gaskets, extruded aluminium frames

The "tough commercial situation" was to provide, in 18 months, accommodation for 750–1,000 employees on reclaimed land of poor load-bearing capacity at a cost comparable to the cheapest temporary structures. The outcome was a permanent building offering higher-quality finishes at half the cost that IBM were spending on headquarters buildings at the time.

After two months, Foster Associates put together a convincing case for a custom-designed deep-plan building with synthesised structure, services and movement patterns. The report also demonstrated that a single-storey envelope would preserve views and trees, provide ample parking space and still allow room for expansion. All services are located in the roof lattice, and structural services and wiring are carried down the hollow steel columns to rectangular "dice" boxes, allowing the interior to respond quickly to growth and change.

Continued

1

2

3

4

IBM has several times availed itself of the inherent flexibility of the building's design. The staff restaurant has been moved and the computer room altered and expanded twice. Although the building was expected to provide only temporary accommodation while permanent headquarters were built on the adjoining site, its ability to respond to changing needs has ensured its survival 25 years after its completion.

5

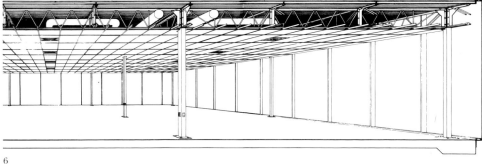

6

1–3   Exterior views
4   Exploded plan
5   Exterior view of glass wall
6   Perspective section

Willis Faber & Dumas

Design/Completion 1970/1975
Ipswich, England
Willis Faber & Dumas Ltd
21,000 square metres
In-situ reinforced concrete structure on piled foundations with
waffle slabs, steel roof structure, suspended structural
glazing system
Exposed concrete, glass, rubber and carpet flooring, steel
partitions, turfed roof

The building's plan form responds to the
medieval street pattern of the old core of
Ipswich by being low and deep, respecting
the scale of the historic town. An outer
necklace of columns forms the perimeter
of the irregular urban site, allowing the
building to follow the curving street plan
without leaving small leftover pockets of
unusable space.

Attention has been paid to providing
a properly integrated, fully democratic
workplace. The two office floors, each
accommodating 600 staff, are fully open
plan. The moving staircases linking all
levels enable visitors to comprehend the
building in a way which is not possible in
conventional office buildings. Leisure, too,
has been incorporated, with an Olympic
size swimming pool on the ground floor,
and a restaurant and roof garden.

The glass sheath that runs around the
building is a system developed in
conjunction with Pilkingtons.

Continued

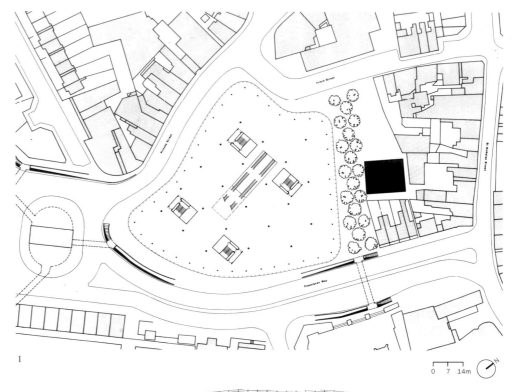

1

0 7 14m

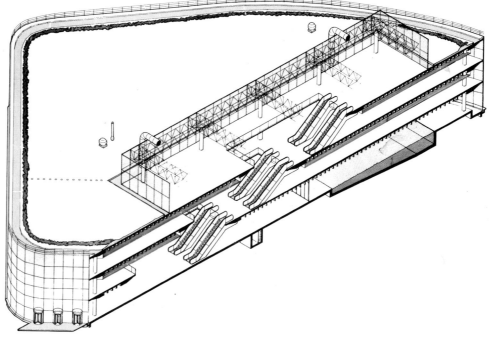

2

3

4

Three-storey-high modules of solar tinted glass are suspended from bolts and a continuous clamping strip, with patch fittings to connect plates of glass and internal fins to provide lateral wind bracing.

By day, the glass reflects a faceted jumble of buildings and sky; by night it dissolves to reveal the internal organs of the building within.

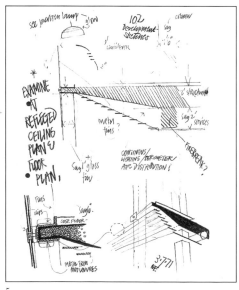

5

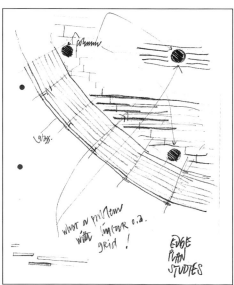

6

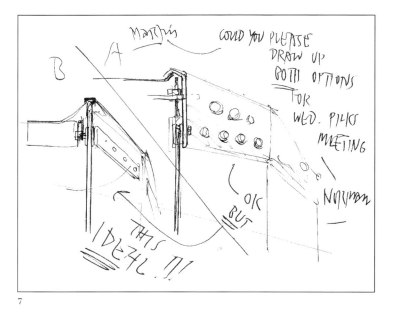

7

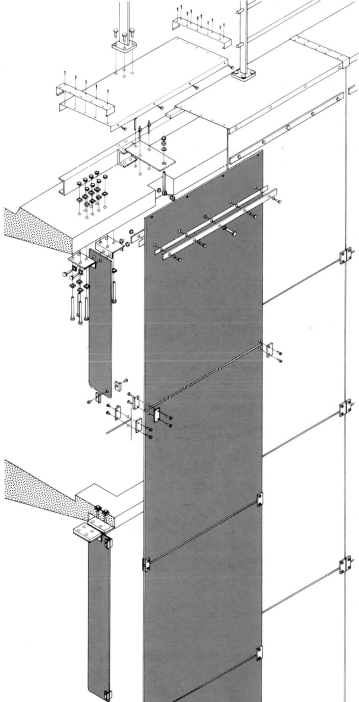

8

4 Exterior view at night
5–7 Development sketches
8 Exploded view of glazing and fixtures

Sainsbury Centre for Visual Arts

Design/Completion 1974/1978
Norwich, England
Sir Robert and Lady Sainsbury/University of East Anglia
6,186 square metres
Steel portal frames, concrete slab
Steel, aluminium cladding, glass end walls, rubber and
carpet flooring

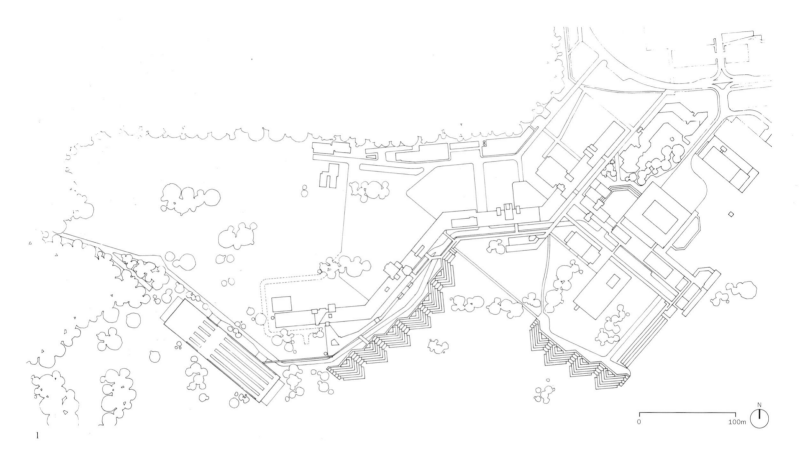

1   Site plan
2   Aerial view
3&4 Concept sketches
5   Exterior view
6   Concept sketch
7   Axonometric section

3

4

5

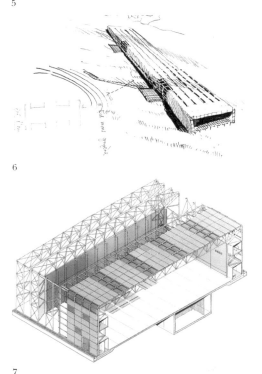

6

7

When Sir Robert and Lady Sainsbury donated their private art collection to the University of East Anglia, together with an endowment fund for a new building to house it, it was decided to enlarge the brief to make the Sainsbury Centre an academic and social focus within the university.

The new building accommodates not only the Sainsbury's collection of primitive and 20th century art and a temporary exhibition space, but also a conservatory, restaurant and senior common room and the Faculty of Fine Art. All these activities are grouped within a single, clear-span structure, glazed at both ends and lit from above by a controlled mixture of natural and artificial light. A basement spine provides the necessary storage and workshop facilities.

The building is divided crosswise by bands of accommodation, all unified by the ceiling—a complex, layered arrangement of grilles, trusses and catwalks. Prismatic towers and trusses house all services,

Continued

toilets and ancillaries as well as providing a freeway for lighting installations and maintenance. The primary steel structure supports a flexible arrangement of solid aluminium or glazed cladding panels. The entire inner wall and ceiling lining is a tuneable system of perforated aluminium louvres. At each end, the steel structure is clearly articulated.

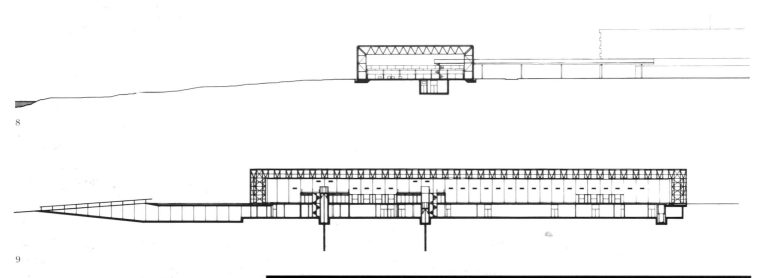

8

9

8   Cross-section
9   Long section
10 Rear service access
11 Main exhibition space
12 Staircase from high walkway
13 Detail cross-section

10

11

12

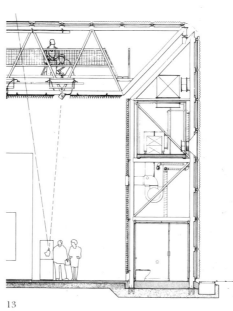

13

Hongkong and Shanghai Banking Corporation Headquarters, Hong Kong

Competition/Completion 1979/1985
Hong Kong
Hongkong and Shanghai Banking Corporation
99,000 square metres
Steel structure, concrete basements
Steel, aluminium cladding, glass, plug-in service modules, stainless steel finishes, aluminium partitions, marble/stone/carpet raised floor

The client's brief to Foster Associates, after they had won the commission in an international competition in 1979, was quite categorical: what was required was nothing less than the best bank building in the world. The site, at the head of Statue Square, is one of the most spectacular in Hong Kong.

The building is suspended from four pairs of steel masts arranged in three bays. At five points up the building, the masts are connected by two-storey trusses from which the floor clusters are suspended. The bays rise to varying heights, creating a staggered profile. The exterior is a vigorously modelled combination of aluminium-clad structure and transparent panels to express the rich mixture of spaces within.

Continued

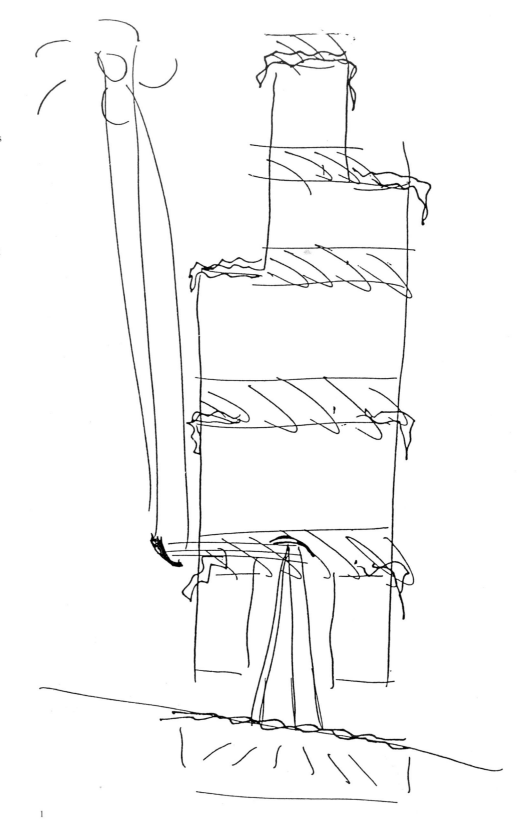

2

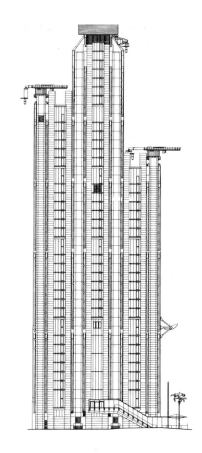

3

4

1 Concept sketch by Norman Foster
2 Bank at night
3 West elevation
4 Section
Following Page:
5 General exterior view

7

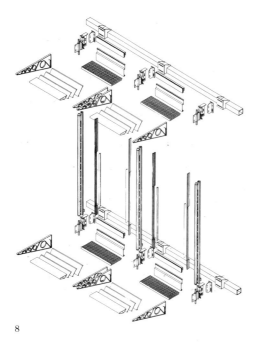

8

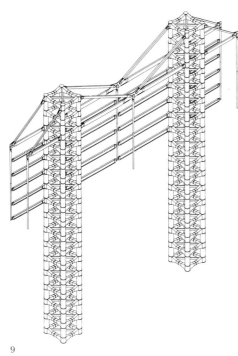

9

10

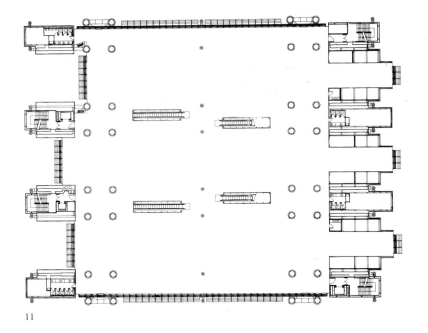

11

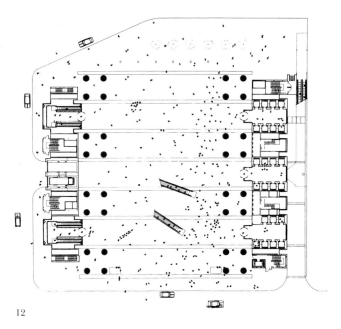

12

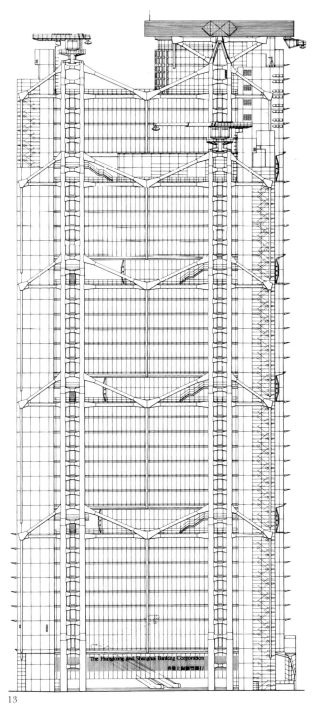

13

The bank building has a public base, a private summit and a central section composed of semi-private and semi-public space.

At street level, a 12-metre-high public pedestrian concourse runs clear beneath the building; a pair of escalators rise up to the main banking hall (semi-public) and its 10-storey atrium. The main body of the bank is reached by three sets of lifts which move at high speed up and down the west elevation in glazed lift shafts. Visitors are set down at each of the double-height levels and complete their journey by escalator.

The flexibility of the spaces within the bank has allowed its entire population to relocate several times since the building opened in 1985. In 1995 a new dealer room was inserted in just six weeks.

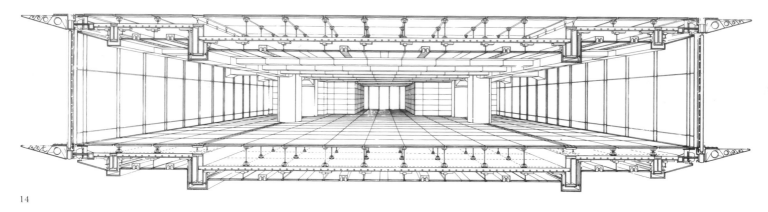

14

15

16

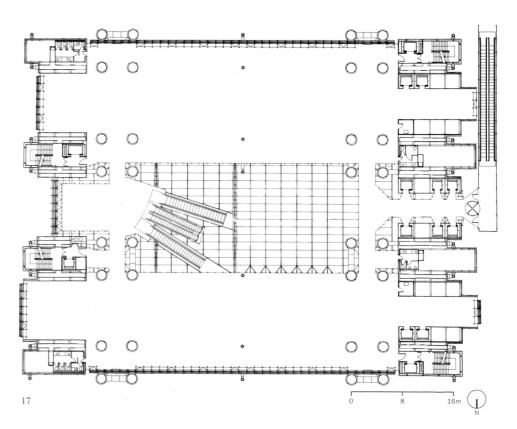

17

0   8   16m

N

18

19

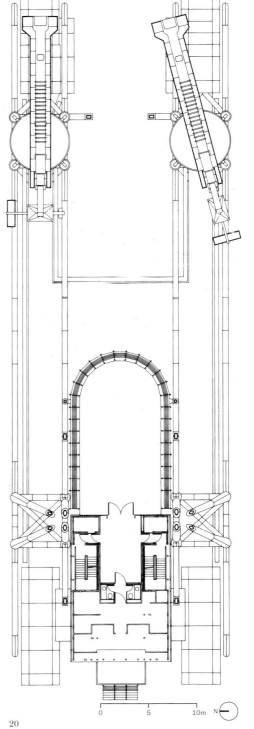

20

0   5   10m N

Renault Distribution Centre

Design/Completion 1980/1983
Swindon, England
Renault UK Ltd
25,000 square metres
Steel structure on reinforced concrete slab
Painted steel, glass, insulated aluminium cladding panels,
rubber flooring

1

The building, which has been described as one of Foster's most playful and has figured prominently in Renault's corporate advertising, stands on an irregular, sloping plot of approximately 6.5 hectares on the western edge of Swindon. The local planners were so delighted with the proposed scheme that they agreed to raise their earlier limit on site development coverage from 50 to 67 per cent, enabling Renault to increase their floor area by 10,000 square metres.

All activities are contained within a single structure made up of modules 24 x 24 metres square in plan, with an internal height of 7.5 metres rising to 9.5 metres at the apex and suspended from 16-metre masts. Forty-two modules accommodate a warehouse, a distribution centre, regional offices, a showroom for cars and trucks, a training school, workshops, a restaurant and an entrance canopy.

Continued

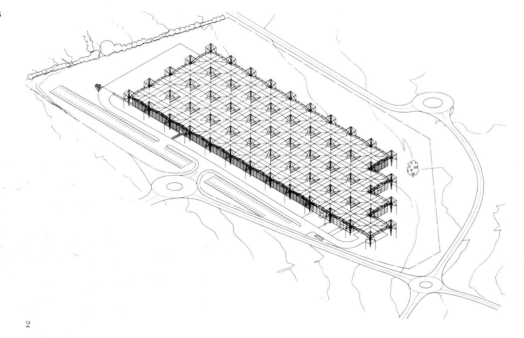

2

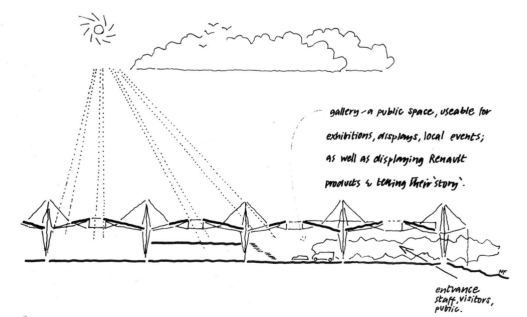

gallery - a public space, useable for exhibitions, displays, local events; as well as displaying Renault products & telling their story.

entrance
staff, visitors,
public.

3

1 Front elevation
2 Axonometric
3 Section sketch
4 Elevation
5 Section structure sketch
6 Entrance canopy

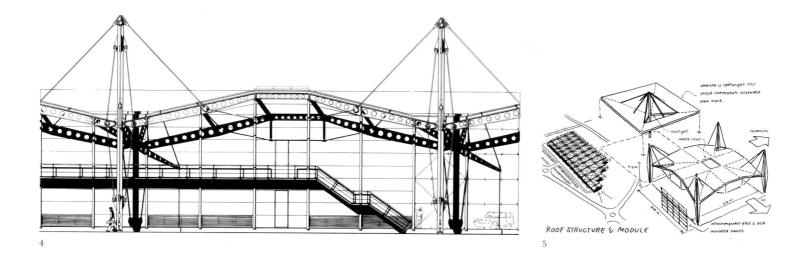

4

5

ROOF STRUCTURE & MODULE

6

7

8

9

10

7   Side view of centre
8   Exterior view through buttercups
9   Long elevation
10   Long section
11   Section through offices, training school and showroom
12   Interior view
13   Ground floor plan

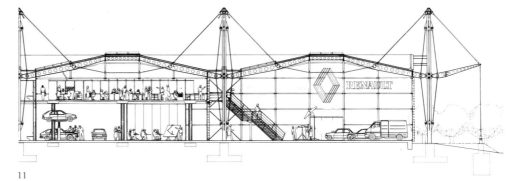

11

The yellow-painted structural steel frame has been carried outside the external wall panels so that its complex assembly of arched steel beams suspended from hollow steel masts can be made plain and visible.

The roof cover, a continuous reinforced PVC membrane, is pierced by clear glass panels at each column, thus combining the benefits of natural top light inside with views of the structural masts and tension rods outside.

12

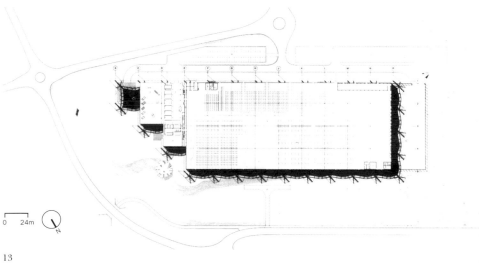

0   24m

13

London's Third Airport, Stansted

Design/Completion 1981/1991
Stansted, Essex, England
BAA Plc
85,700 square metres
Painted steel structural "trees" and steel roof shells with concrete floor slabs
Steel, glass, concrete, granite, stainless steel

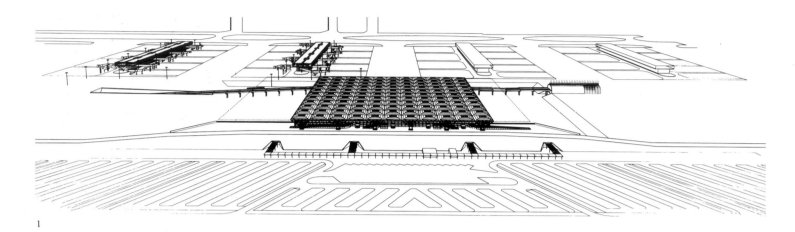

1

The Foster master plan for Stansted returned to the basics of early airports: the runway, the terminal and the approach road.

Movement through the terminal building is straight, unimpeded and on one level; all services, baggage handling and rail links are banished to an undercroft, leaving the concourse as a clear, logical zone through which passengers proceed towards departure lounges and thence to shuttle links with the satellite buildings.

By putting all the services normally housed on the roof under the concourse, the roof is then able to admit and reflect light. Tubular steel structural "trees" support the continuous roof canopy. Natural light floods in through the glazed side walls and through apertures in the roof, while artificial light bounces off the reflective underside of the domed roof shells. The form of the terminal is only slightly higher than the mature trees on the site, yet it retains a strong and recognizable presence by night as well as by day.

Not only was the Stansted terminal cheaper per square metre than any previous British air terminal building and its running costs 50 per cent lower, it was also the first terminal to take the environment into consideration.
By digging the bulk of the building into the site (an important energy saving measure), the impact on the surrounding landscape was kept to a minimum.

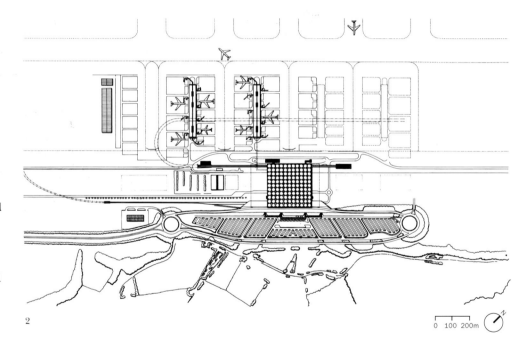

2

0 100 200m

1   Terminal zone perspective
2   Terminal zone master plan
3   Drop-off road
4   Eaves detail

3

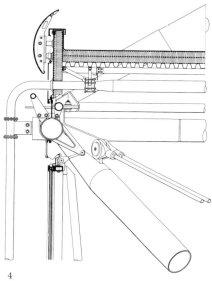

4

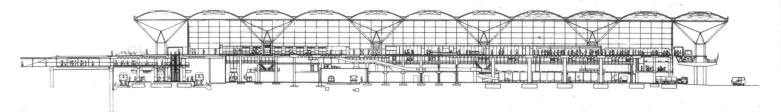

5

6

5 Section
6 Entrance canopy
7 Night view
8 Concourse plan
9 Baggage reclaim area

7

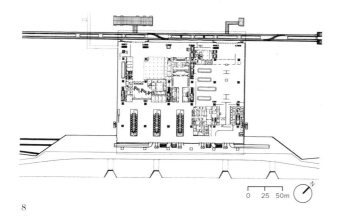

8

9

10

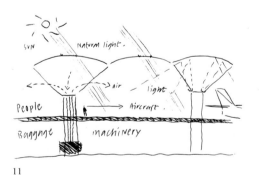

11

12

13

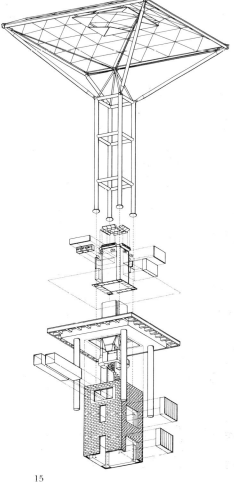

15

14

10   Interior view
11   Concept sketch by Norman Foster
12   Detail of information pod
13   Sunlight through roof
14   View of roof shell and lights
15   Tree and services pod

BBC Radio Headquarters

Design 1982–1985
London, England
British Broadcasting Corporation
52,000 square metres
Reinforced concrete frame
Natural stone cladding, translucent glass panels, clear glass,
exposed concrete

This project was the brainchild of the then chairman of the BBC, Lord Howard, who held an international competition, which Foster Associates won in 1982. Although it exists to provide public service broadcasting, the BBC is a surprisingly introverted organisation. Close consultation with the BBC resulted in a series of briefs to unravel and open up the Corporation.

The proposals stressed the importance of the BBC's public responsibilities in broadcasting by carving diagonally into the site to create a huge glazed atrium—fully open to the public—on the axis of All Souls Church.

A structural grid laid across this axis produced a neat geometry, with the resulting diagonal grid subdivided into zones of studio space flanked by strips of circulation and services. The diagonal geometry also made it easier for the building to respond to its historic context.

Continued

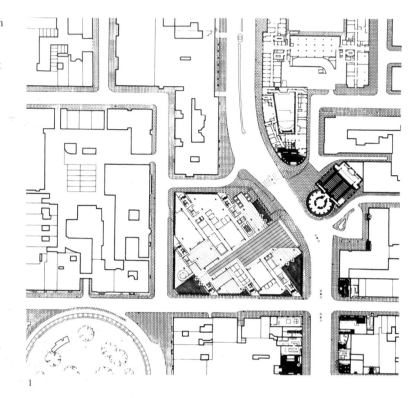

1

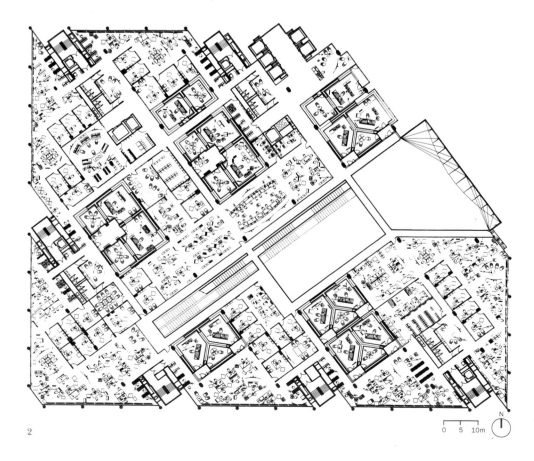

2

0   5   10m

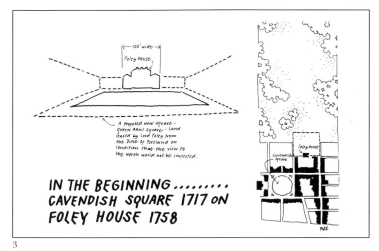

IN THE BEGINNING.........
CAVENDISH SQUARE 1717 ON
FOLEY HOUSE 1758

3

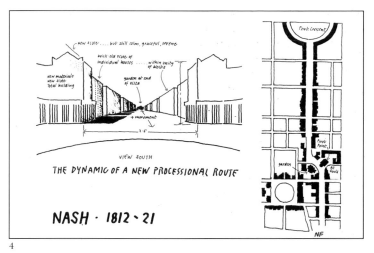

VIEW SOUTH

THE DYNAMIC OF A NEW PROCESSIONAL ROUTE

NASH · 1812·21

4

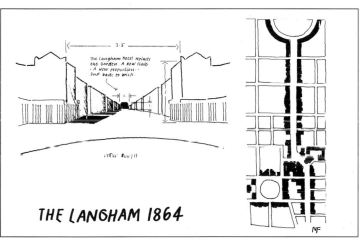

THE LANGHAM 1864

5

1920'S TO NOW

6

1   Ground level plan
2   Typical floor plan
3–6   Site analysis sketches

8

7   View from All Souls to atrium
8   Aerial view of model

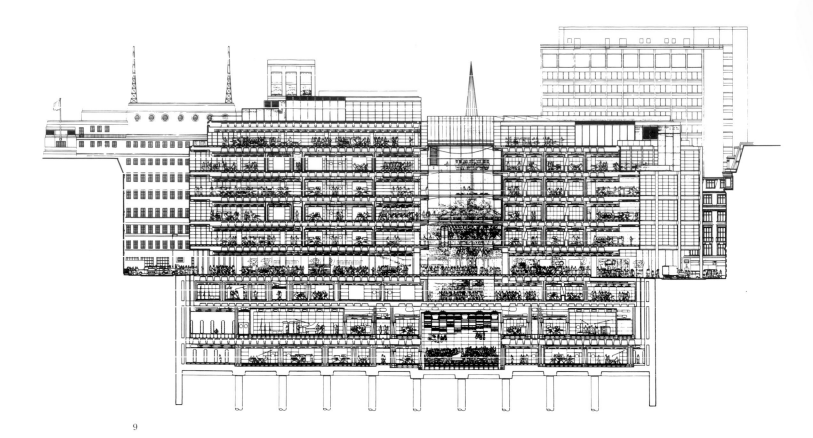

9

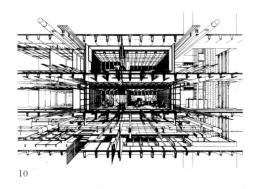

10

9   Cross-section through atrium
10 Sectional perspective of studio
11 Model view of atrium
12 Section through atrium
13 Elevation onto Cavendish Square

11

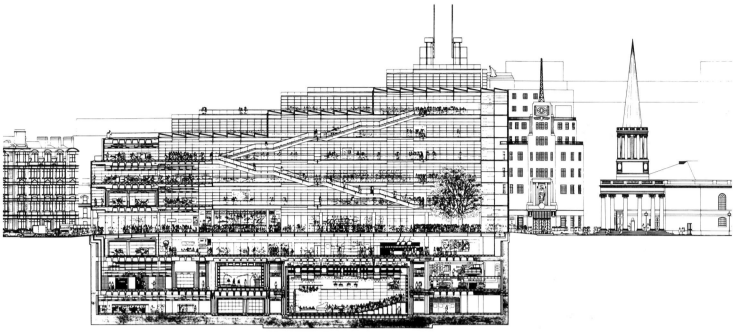

12

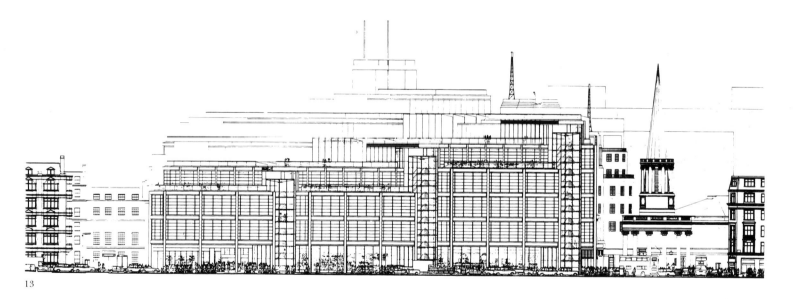

13

A low elevation faced Cavendish Square to the south-west, and rose to a climax of glass lift towers on the north-east elevation to Portland Place.

The design emerged from the need to solve three contextual problems with one building: the context of Cavendish Square, the need for a punctuation mark at the southern end of Portland Place and a complicated relationship on the S-bend of the street with All Souls and Broadcasting House, all part of Nash's great processional route.

Carré d'Art

Competition/Completion 1984/1993
Nîmes, France
Ville de Nîmes
18,000 square metres
Concrete frame
Exposed concrete; clear, opaque and translucent glass;
canvas; stainless steel; stone

The challenge in designing the Carré d'Art at Nîmes—a complex containing a museum of contemporary art and a médiathèque, or public library—was to design a building which could stand up to the powerful historic presence of the Maison Carrée which stands opposite it. The Maison is one of the finest examples of a Roman temple in France and is in a miraculous state of preservation. The design has also been influenced by the vernacular architecture of the region, with its cool courtyards, steps and terraces, and the Roman grid pattern of the city centre.

The Carré d'Art attempts to combine these themes in a modern way. Half of its nine-storey structure is buried below ground in order to respect surrounding building heights. At its heart, a five-storey internal courtyard exploits the lightness and transparency of modern materials, especially clear, translucent and opaque glass.

Continued

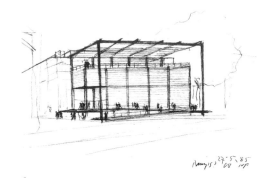

1

2

3

1   Concept sketch by Norman Foster
2   View of Carré d'Art through columns
    of Maison Carrée
3   Exterior view
4   Night view with Maison Carrée in foreground
5   Activities in front of the centre at night

4

5

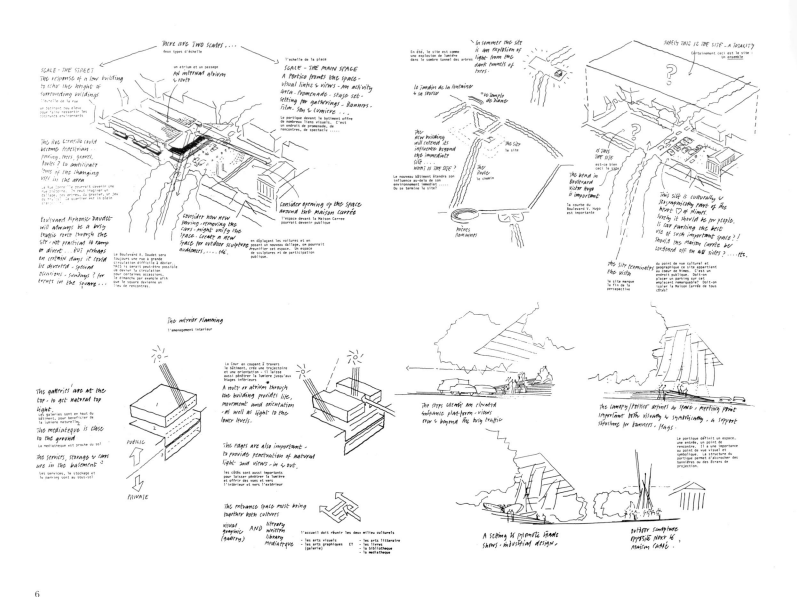

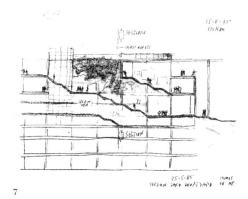

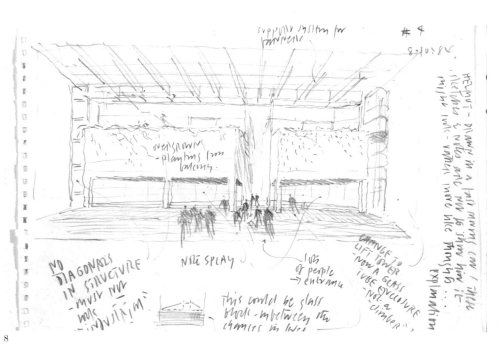

6

7

8

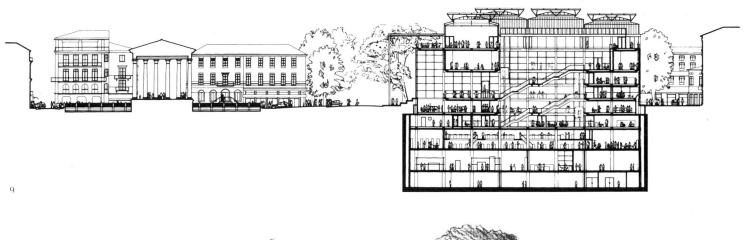

9

10

11

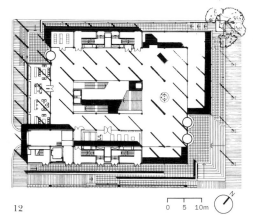

12

13

6   Concept and site analysis sketches
    by Norman Foster
7   Cross-section sketch
8   Original competition sketch
9   Long section
10 Sectional sketch
11 Interior view
12 Ground level plan
13 View from Carré d'Art to Maison Carrée

14

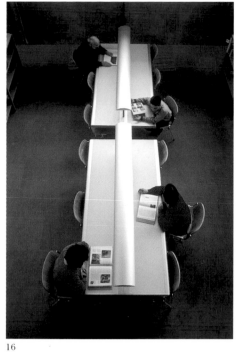

15

16

17

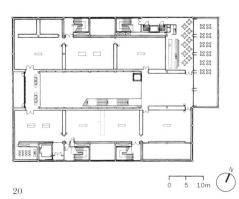

18

19

The art galleries enjoy controlled natural lighting at the top of the building. The library occupies the floors immediately above and below ground level, and is easily accessible from the street. The basement includes a cinema auditorium and conference facilities.

An integral part of the Carré d'Art project was the creation of a new public space in front of the building. By excluding or re-routing traffic, the new paved space was extended around the Maison Carrée and has become a lively new forum or meeting place for the city.

14&15   Library
16   Library tables designed by Foster and Partners
17   Gallery
18   Children's Library
19   View from rooftop café
20   Top gallery and café level

20

0 5 10m

Street Furniture for Decaux

Design/Production 1989/1991
J. C. Decaux
Cast iron, mild steel tube, aluminium panels
Toughened glass and laminated safety glass

1

The quality of street furniture is an important indicator of the health of a city. The litter bin, a proliferating species, can sometimes be as unsightly as the litter it is supposed to collect. Benches and bollards can be a source of delight or dismay, depending on the care with which they have been designed and maintained.

For the French firm J. C. Decaux, Foster Associates developed a bus shelter system based on two structural poles and glass panels. This is an updated version of the Colonne Morris—a rotating advertising drum with an elliptical attachment incorporating grit bins, benches, lavatories, a roof canopy and electronic information systems, and a city boundary sign.

One thousand bus shelters have already been installed in Paris. Others have been installed worldwide in cities as far apart as New York and Bordeaux. Work is currently under way on street lighting designs.

2

4

5

6

The Diploma Galleries, renamed the
Sackler Galleries, follow the plan of the
original ones but have been completely
rebuilt with barrel-vaulted ceilings,
uniform floor levels and a range of
environmental controls. They are reached
via a glazed reception area incorporating
a parapet along which sculpture from the
Academy's permanent collection is
displayed (most notably Michelangelo's
Tondo of the Virgin and Child with the
Infant St John).

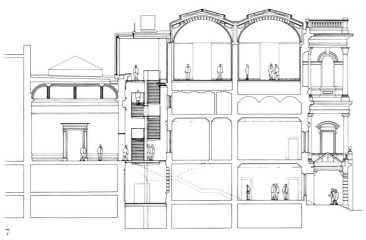

7

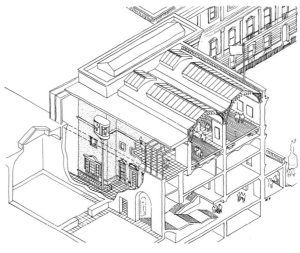

8

9

10

11

4   Long section through "gap"
5   Restored facade behind glass staircase
6   Glass staircase
7   Cross-section through Burlington House
8   Cutaway sketch by Norman Foster
9   Sculpture shelf
10 Michelangelo's tondo
11 Interior view of galleries

Shop for Katharine Hamnett

Design/Completion 1986
Brompton Road, London
Katharine Hamnett/Aguecheek
500 square metres
Existing two-storey garage
Steel, glass, stainless steel

A former car repair workshop, accessible from the street via a gloomy tunnel, was transformed into a spacious showroom for fashion designer Katharine Hamnett.

Light and space were the main ingredients: the quality of natural light from the roof and the translucent windows was enhanced by white finishes, generous use of mirrors and an absence of clutter, reminiscent of a ballet school or a sculptor's studio.

The entrance passageway was transformed by the insertion of a bridge of etched glass panels, which arches and meanders towards the white-painted space beyond.

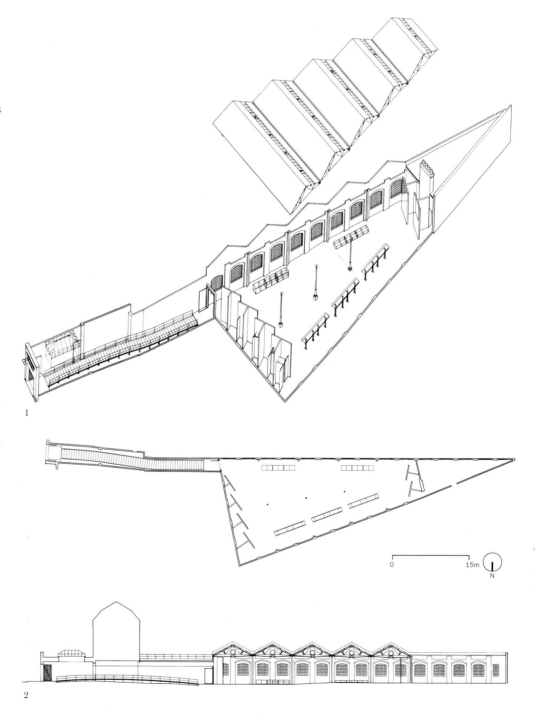

1

2

3

4

5

6

7

Century Tower

Design/Completion 1987/1991
Tokyo, Japan
Obunsha Corporation
26,590 square metres
Electro-slag-welded steel box structure
Steel, glass, aluminium, stainless steel, stone, carpet

Century Tower, Foster Associates' first building in Tokyo, occupies a site governed by complex zoning regulations and strict seismic and fire protection codes. The design response has been to divide the block into two towers (19 and 21 storeys high), linked by a full-height atrium slot. The atrium permits natural light to flood into the heart of the building. Narrow bridges link the two towers and enable tenants, should they so wish, to occupy whole floors.

The other key element is the double-height floor system, with mezzanine floors suspended from the huge, eccentrically braced structural frame. Lifts and services have been pulled to the periphery, leaving column-free office space with natural light and dramatic views.

Continued

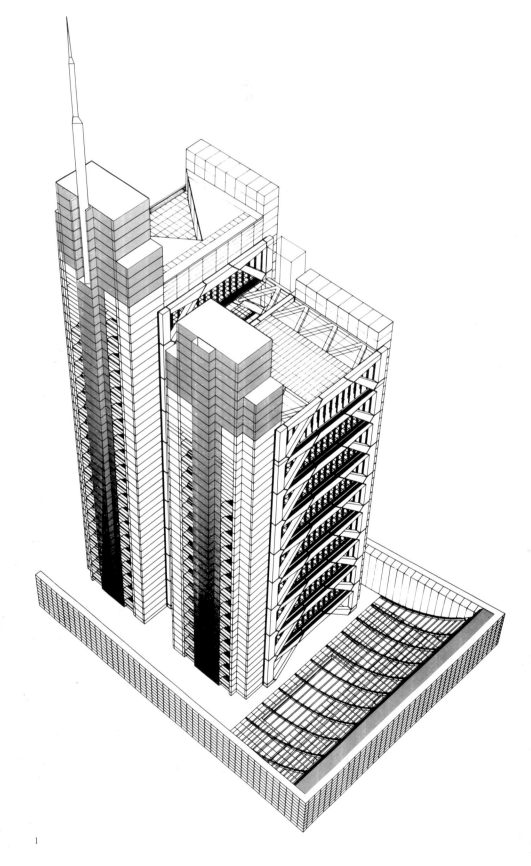

1   CAD perspective
2   Entrance by night

1

2

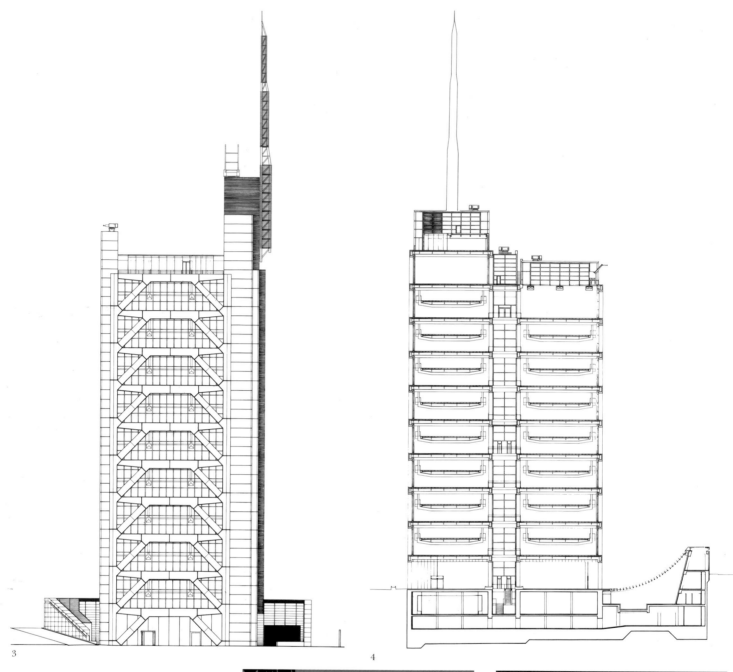

3

4

5

6

7

8

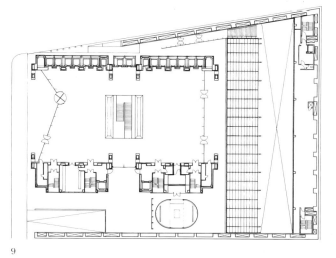

9

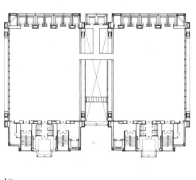

10

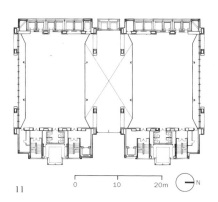

11

0   10   20m

N

The double-height entrance lobby leads
to a restaurant beneath a glass roof whose
curved underside recalls Japanese temple
design. On a level below, there is a health
club and a museum housing the client's
collection of Asian art and artefacts.
The building thus caters for a wide range
of uses. Public areas—a traditional tea
house and the museum—are incorporated
with the private realm of club, restaurant,
pools and gym.

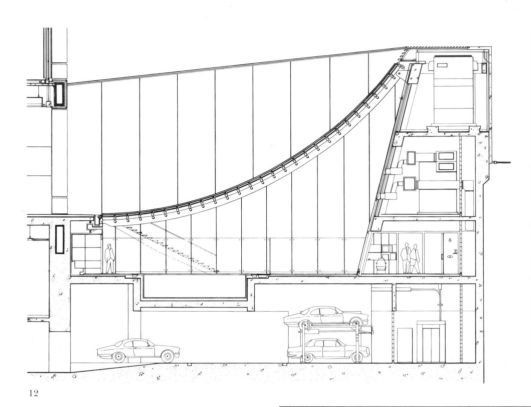

12

13

12   Section through catenary roof
13   Restaurant under catenary roof
14   Basement museum
15   Fitness centre
16   Fitness centre swimming pool

14

15

16

Houses in Japan

Design/Completion 1987/1992
Japan
Main house: 600 square metres
Guest house: 400 square metres
Steel structure, timber decking
Steel, timber, sisal matting, stainless steel, glass,
aluminium louvres, silk wall panels

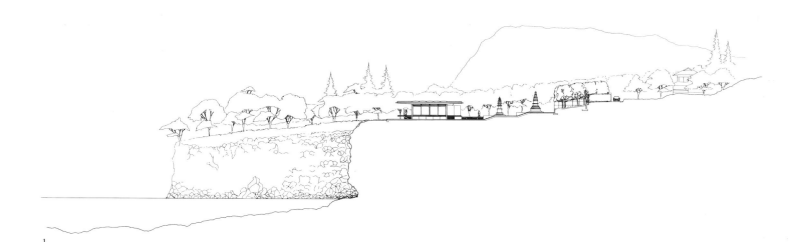

1

In designing these houses in Japan,
Foster Associates united two traditions:
the Japanese love of harmony and respect
for nature and the Western obsession with
the dematerialised architecture of the
pristine steel and glass box. It was the
client's wish that the houses should take
their inspiration from traditional Japanese
design.

The main house and its adjoining guest
house are sited on a dramatic stretch of
volcanic coastline with long, inaccessible
fingers of rock jutting out into the sea.
The main house floats above ground on
a raised deck and has been positioned so
that the entrance lobby and main living
room enjoy uninterrupted views out to sea.

Continued

2

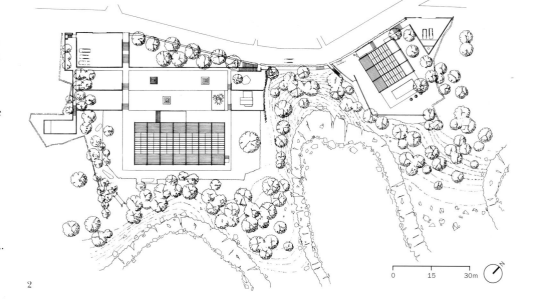

3

1 Main house site section
2 Site plan
3 Interior/exterior

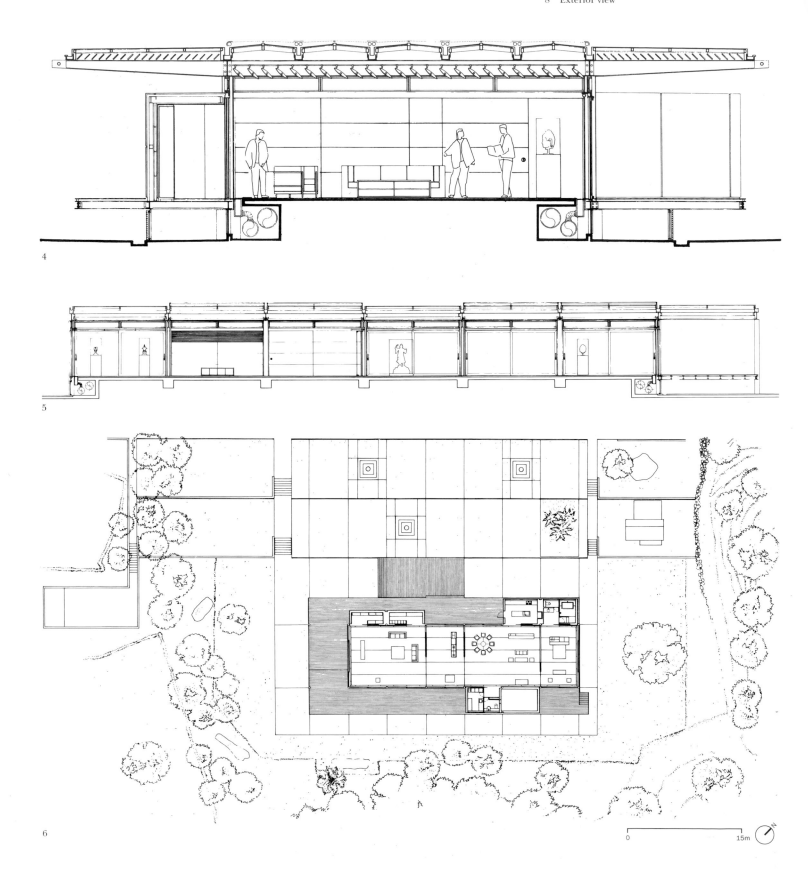

4

5

6

0   15m

The structure of both houses is the same: regular bays made up of cantilevered steel frames. In each bay, between the columns, sliding, double-height, glazed doors lead onto the decks which are themselves protected from sunlight by fixed louvres. Internally, the space can be similarly modified by means of sliding screens, while the quality of top lighting provided by the glass roof can be changed by manipulating the insulated ceiling louvres. The internal services and storage areas are arranged around the exterior, allowing more flexible use of the central living space.

7

8

American Air Museum

Design/Completion 1987/1997
Duxford, England
Imperial War Museum
7,400 square metres
Precast concrete roof structure, in-situ concrete base structure
Concrete, stainless steel, glass wall, steel mullions

Duxford airfield, 13 kilometres south of Cambridge, was a Battle of Britain fighter station and now houses the Imperial War Museum's collection of historic aircraft. Links with the United States have always been strong: in 1918 some 200 US airmen were stationed at Duxford, and between 1943 and 1945 it was the headquarters for one of more than 100 US airforce bases in Britain.

Duxford's collection of 38 American planes—19 of which still fly—is probably the finest outside the US. The largest of these, a B-52 bomber, forms the centrepiece of the new American Air Museum, and its giant dimensions (61-metre wing span and 16-metre-high tail fin) have largely determined the form of the building.

With a ground plan recalling the nose cone of an aircraft, the structure, measuring 90 x 100 metres, is partly sunk into the ground. Its most striking features are the wide and gently curving roof and the fully glazed end elevation, incorporating the largest single glazed panels in manufacture. The complex geometry of the roof structure—wide spanning arches at one end developing into a shallow dome at the rear—means that it can be made up of only five components, specially cast on site.

1

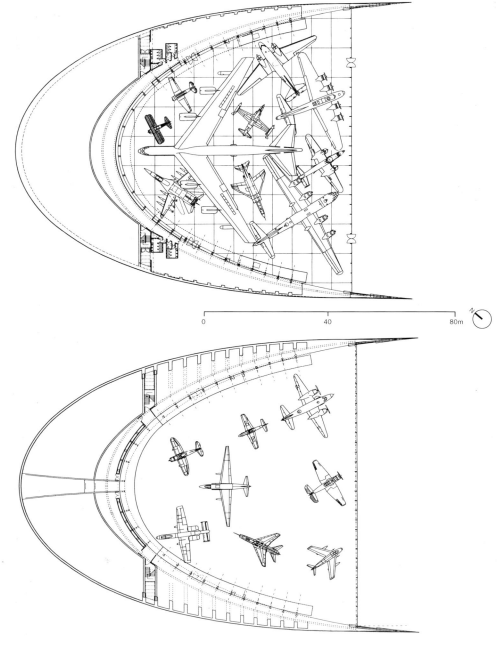

1   Model view
2   Plans
3   Exterior
4&5 Interiors

2

3

4

5

King's Cross Master Plan

Competition 1987
London, England
London Regeneration Consortium
52 hectares

Much of the 52-hectare, largely derelict
site at King's Cross is at present used as
a freight interchange, with assorted
industrial uses and several unused
buildings alongside housing, a canal and
a natural park. It is London's largest
public transport interchange, with two
world famous main line termini (King's
Cross and St Pancras) above ground, a
massive London Transport interchange
below ground, and British Rail's proposed
second terminal for the Channel tunnel
rail link.

The master plan has been created as a
framework within which more detailed
design work could take place.
Five considerations gave rise to the
organisation of the site: a series of heritage
buildings grouped around the historic
railway sheds to the south and the canal/
road interchange in the centre; the canal
itself, which threads through the site; the
transport infrastructure of road and rail;

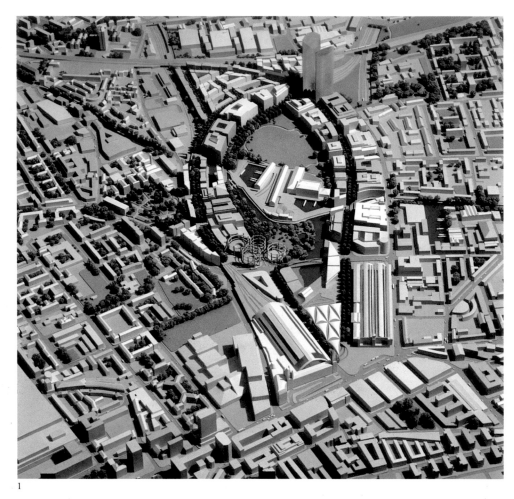

1

2

3

4

5

the need to break down physical barriers around the site and form intelligible new routes; and, at the heart of the development, a new open space in the tradition of London's parks and squares.

The new international terminal was placed between King's Cross and St Pancras stations, its form a vast triangular structure and its glass and steel roof shells admitting the daylight. Its features included unimpeded lines of sight, clear signing, reduced walking distances and smooth changes in level.

Crescent Wing, Sainsbury Centre for Visual Arts

Design/Completion 1988/1991
Norwich, England
University of East Anglia
3,000 square metres
Concrete structure, turfed roof
Glass and aluminium curtain wall, carpet, metal partitions,
plasterboard

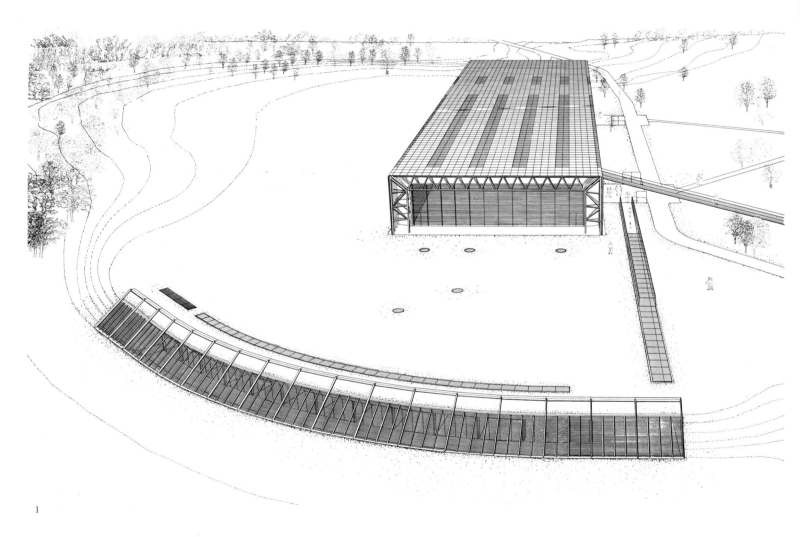

1

The Sainsbury Centre was conceived
as an open-ended building but the
decision to extend it created a dilemma
for both architect and client. A major new
benefaction from Sir Robert and Lady
Sainsbury provided an opportunity for
much-needed additional space for offices,
workshops and the proper display of the
Sainsbury Centre's reserve collection.

The form of the Sainsbury Centre implies
linear growth but the Centre's founders,
Sir Robert and Lady Sainsbury, saw it as
a finite object, perfect in itself. The most
logical course, therefore, was to extend
the building below ground. It made sense
to extend the basement area, especially
as falls in the site would allow the
extended basement to emerge naturally
into the open, with a glazed frontage to
the lake. Study collections and workshops
fit into a rectangular continuation of the

Continued

1 Aerial perspective
2 Long section
3 Site plan
4 Crescent Wing at night

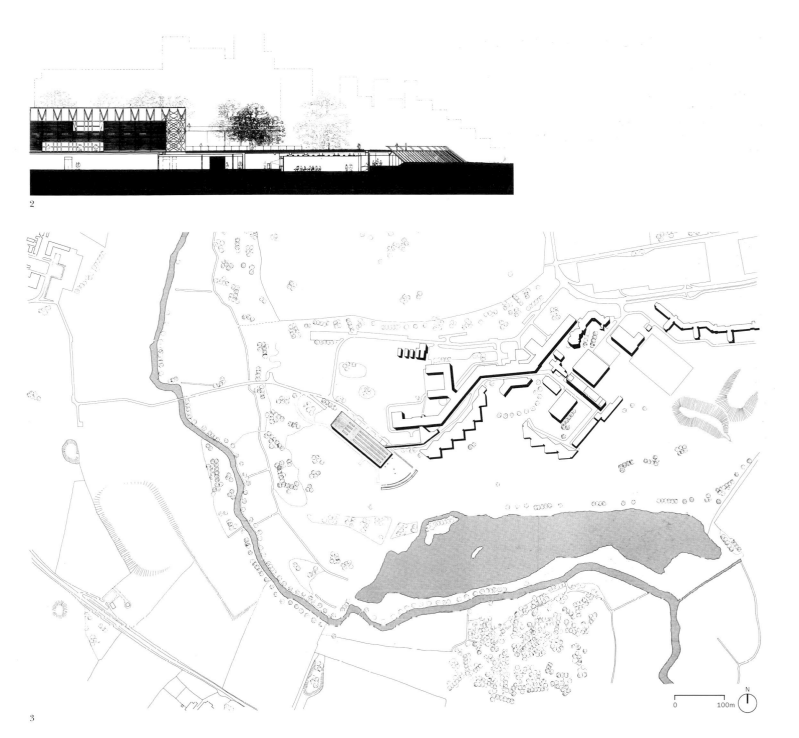

2

3

4

5

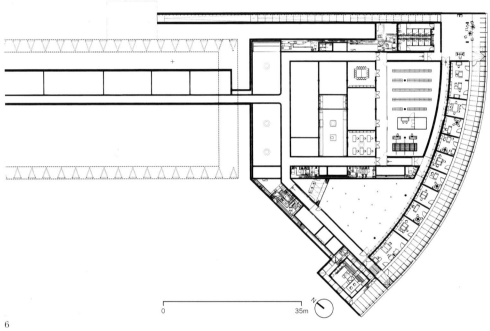

6

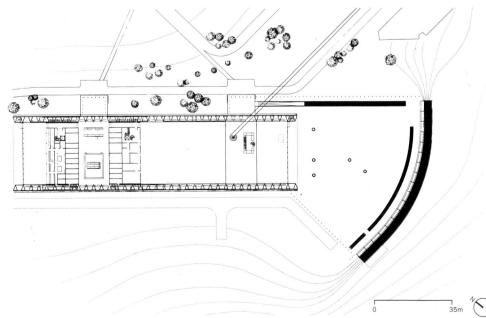

5   View of Sainsbury Centre and Crescent Wing
6   Ground level plan
7   Plan of Sainsbury Centre and Crescent Wing
     grass roof
8   Study reserve detail
9   Section through new wing
10   Study reserve

7

Sainsbury Centre below ground, with offices fanning out to the south away from the Centre.

The exterior gives little hint of what lies beneath. A lawn, punctuated by rooflights, and a narrow side ramp disappearing under the turf provide a clue, but only from the lake is the full extent of the wing apparent, in a great sweep of inclined planes of fritted glass.

8

10

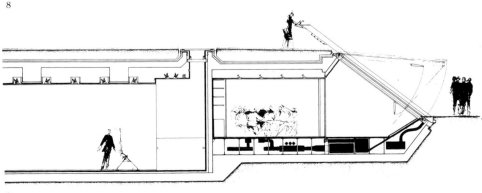

9

Bilbao Metro System

Competition/Completion 1988/1995
Bilbao, Spain
Basque Government/IMEBISA
61 kilometres long
13,000 square metres
Precast concrete panels
Concrete, stainless steel, glass, terrazzo

An underground system is essentially
a series of stations linked by tunnels but
it can rapidly degenerate into a confusing,
ill-maintained and potentially dangerous
labyrinth.

The guiding principle behind the design
for the new Bilbao Metro railway was the
need to strip the problem down to its
essentials. At street level, the metro
is announced by curved glass enclosures
which admit natural light by day and are
illuminated by night. Below, the 16-metre-
wide station caverns, which form the heart
of the system, are reached as simply and
directly as possible by escalators or glass
lifts. The cavern form, a direct engineered
response to the forces of nature,
is celebrated rather than disguised
in the design of the stations.

Continued

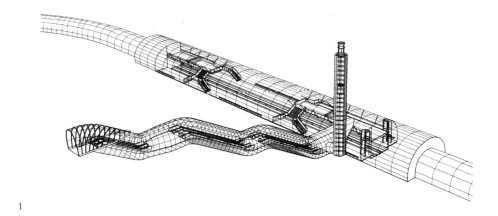

1

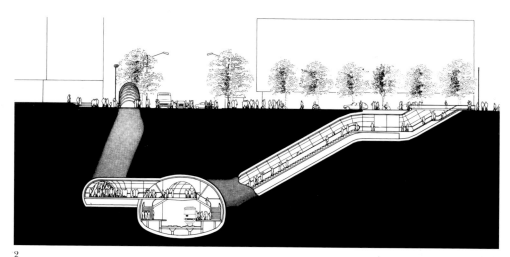

2

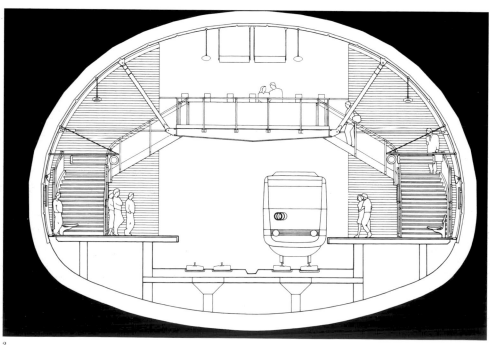

3

1   Diagrammatic cutaway view of typical station
2&3 Cross-section through typical station
4   Fosterito
5   Interior view of station

4

5

6

7

8

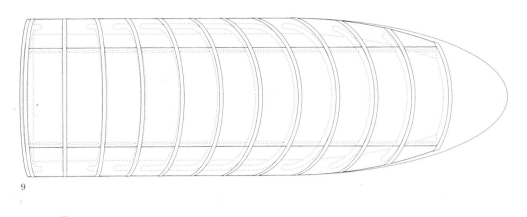

9

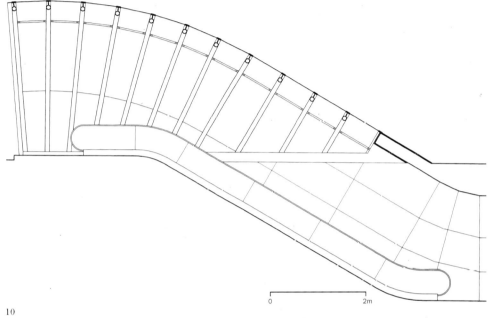

10

11

12

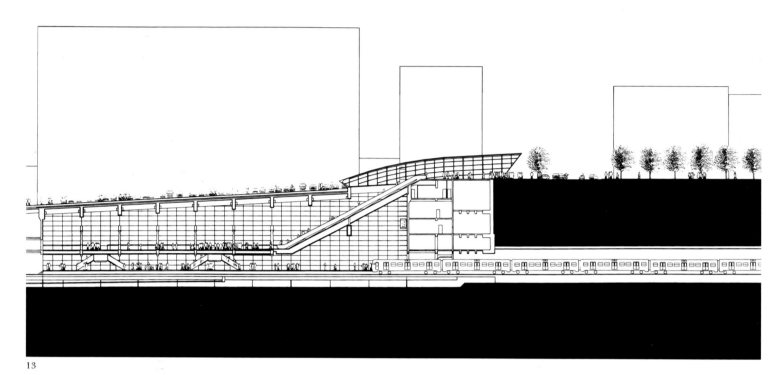

13

14

The lightweight and maintenance-free prefabricated components are treated as separate elements and make a strong contrast with the precast concrete walls of the cavern. All services are confined to plugs at the ends of the caverns. Ventilation ducts and electrical cables run below the platforms and trains are powered by an overhead system.

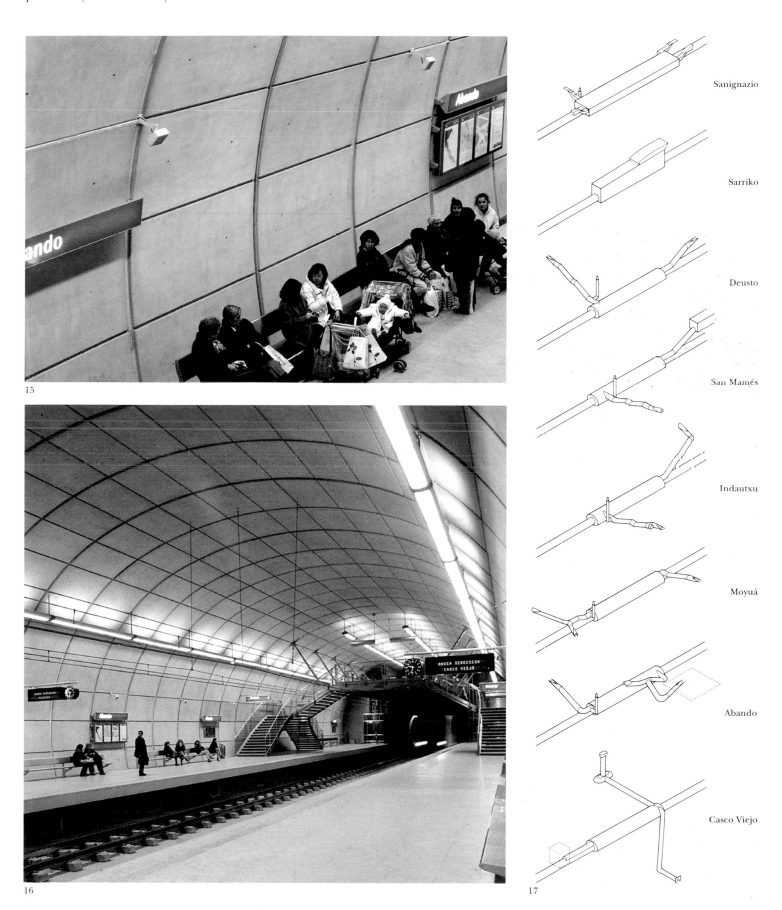

15

16

17

Sanignazio

Sarriko

Deusto

San Mamés

Indautxu

Moyuá

Abando

Casco Viejo

Torre de Collserola

Competition/Completion 1988/1992
Barcelona, Spain
Torre de Collserola SA
288 metres tall
Steel and concrete
Steel, concrete, stainless steel, glass

The rising demand for telecommunications has produced a new form of landscape clutter: the telecommunications tower. The skylines of many major western cities now bristle with these intrusive structures and the free play of market forces has allowed them to proliferate more or less unchecked. In Barcelona, Mayor Pasqual Maragall wished to abolish all masts, towers and microwave dishes from the mountains of Tibidabo and replace them with a single, elegant structure which would respect the surroundings and give the public an opportunity to view the city from a new angle.

Continued

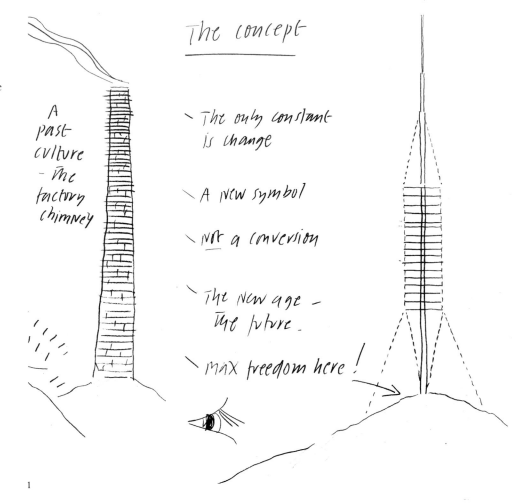

1

2

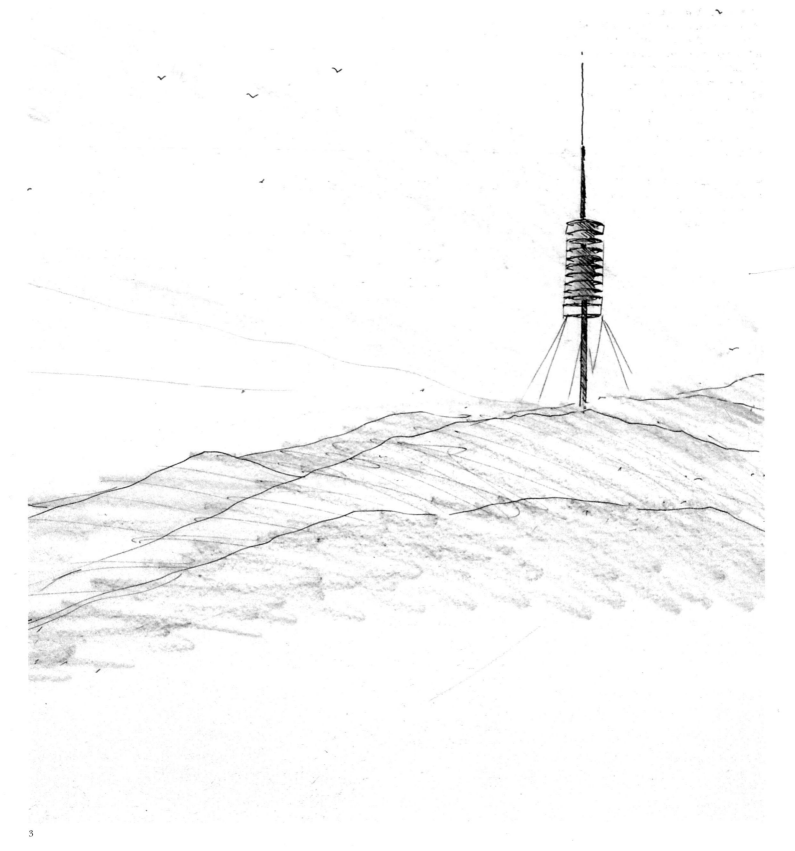

3

4

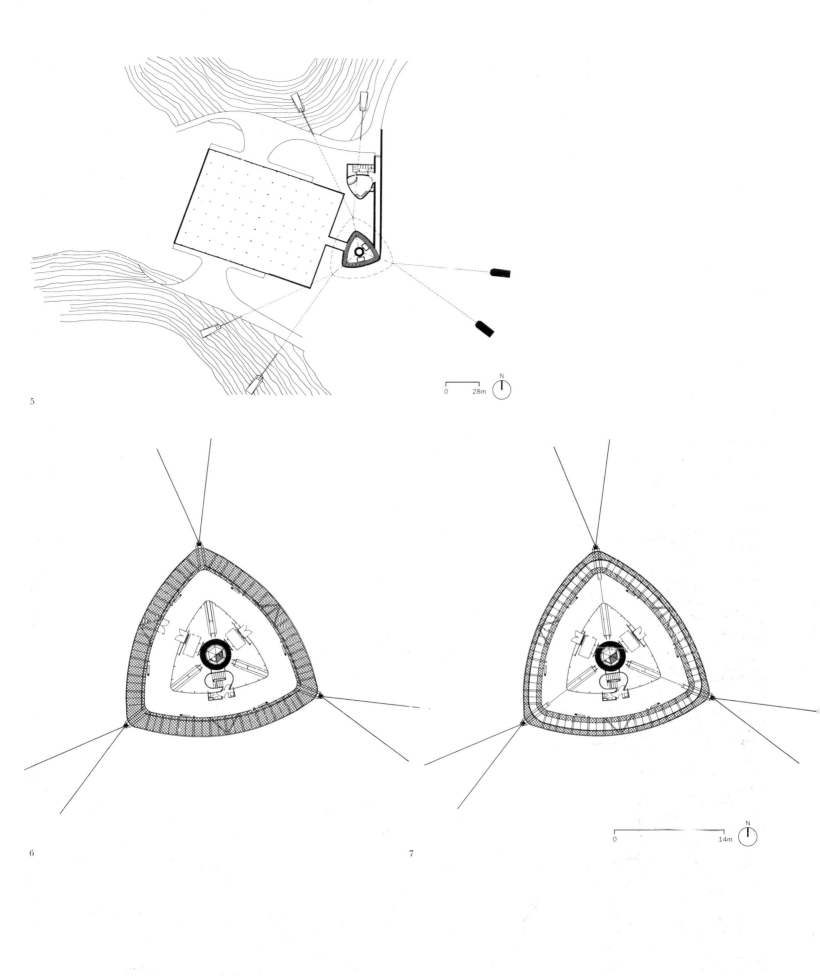

5

6   7

4   View from base of tower
5   Ground level plan
6   Level 8
7   Level 10 viewing platform

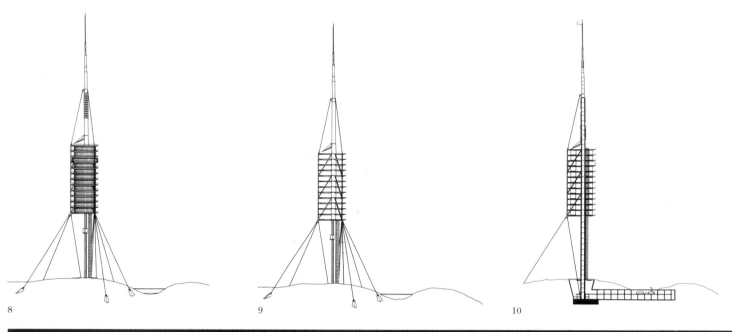

8   9   10

11

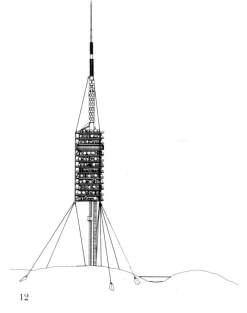

12

The competition-winning design was for
a 288-metre tower with a main shaft of
only 4.5 metres in diameter, tapering
to a 300-millimetre diameter radio mast.
Thirteen main floors, surrounded by
a perimeter of open stainless steel grilles,
are suspended from the shaft by three
primary trusses; the structure is tethered
to the mountainside by three pairs of guys
made from pretensioned steel cable.
The tower was completed in time for the
Barcelona Olympics in 1992 and has since
become a symbol for the city.

13

14

15

8   Structure and cladding
9   Structure
10   Section
11   View at night
12   Structure, cladding and satellite dishes
13   Exterior view at dusk
14   General view of tower looking up
15   View of tower

ITN Headquarters

Design/Completion 1988/1990
London, England
Independent Television News/Stanhope Properties
41,000 square metres
Concrete structure
Concrete, stainless steel, aluminium, glass, stone

The site, on Gray's Inn Road, London, had recently been vacated by the Times newspaper. It presented a number of challenges to a company determined to open up the news gathering process. The most important of these was the vast basement area in which the old newspaper printing presses had been sited. Some of the underground space could be used for television studios, but much was unlit and unusable. The solution was to punch through the ground floor slab to admit light into the basement. This formed the basis of a full-height atrium, capped by a glazed canopy, which became the focus for the interior of the building.

The high insulation levels achieved by the cladding are the key to the energy savings made in this building. The double-layer glazed walls have an unusually deep cavity of 350 millimetres between them,

Continued

1

2

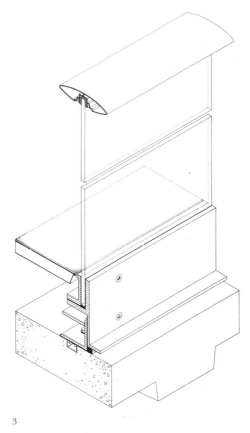

3

4

5

providing an insulating layer of air around
the whole building. Return air from the
air-conditioning system is collected at the
base of the double-glazed wall. It is then
sucked up through the cavity and through
ducts in the ceiling for reheating or
cooling.

The building has now become
synonymous with the image of the
company, forming the backdrop to its
news broadcasts. In addition, the
customised studios, originally created for
ITN's sole use, are now profitably leased to
the television industry at large.

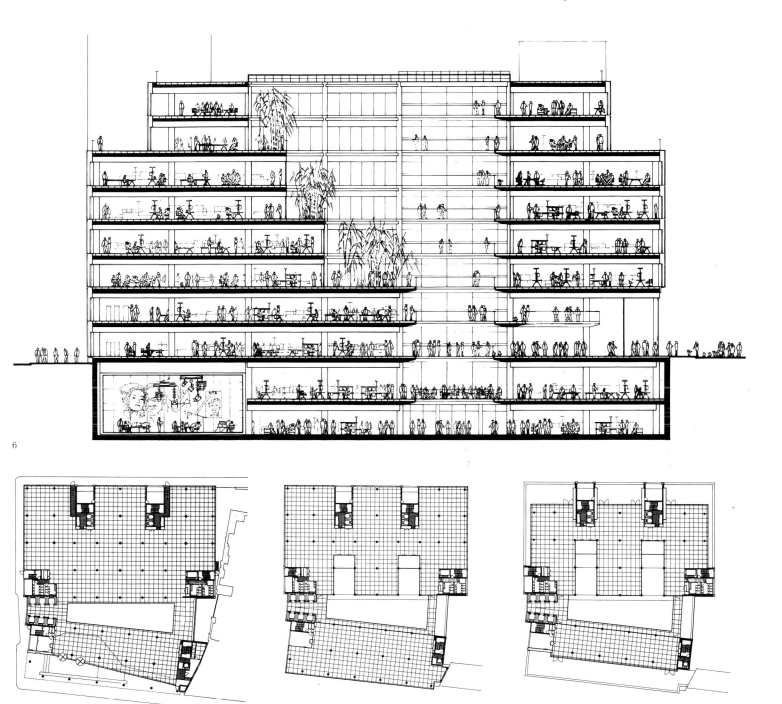

3   Handrail detail
4   News studio in open atrium
5   View across atrium to open studio
6   East–west cross-section
7   Ground level plan
8   Level 3 plan
9   Level 7 plan

6

7

8

9

0   9m

Business Promotion Centre

Design/Completion 1988/1993
Duisburg, Germany
GTT/Kaiser Bautechnik
4,000 square metres
Concrete frame
Exposed concrete, suspended glass wall, carpet, stainless
steel, stone, plasterboard

The eight-storey Business Promotion
Centre is intended as a landmark building
to revive business and promote social
change in the Ruhr area. It was the result
of a particularly creative collaboration with
Kaiser Bautechnik, the environmental
engineers and pioneers of energy-efficient
building systems.

The building is lens-shaped in plan, with
a steel roof curving down over its three
terraced upper floors. At ground level,
the entrance extends into a double-height
banking and exhibition hall. The floors
in between are a combination of cellular
offices and meeting spaces, culminating
in a grand internal three-storey terrace.

The energy needs of the building are met
by a combination of two types of solar cell
mounted on the roof. Photovoltaic cells
convert the sun's energy into electric
power, while solar panels heat water,
which is fed to an absorption cooler for
the radiant cooling system. Both of these
subsidise the energy required by the
building's gas-powered cogenerator and
enable the owner to make a profit on the
energy sold to the tenants.

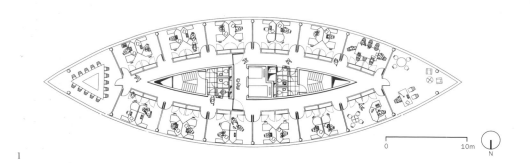

1

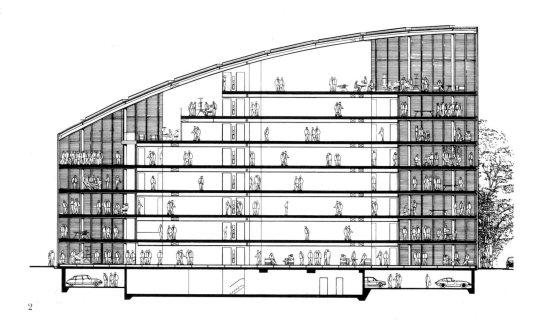

2

3

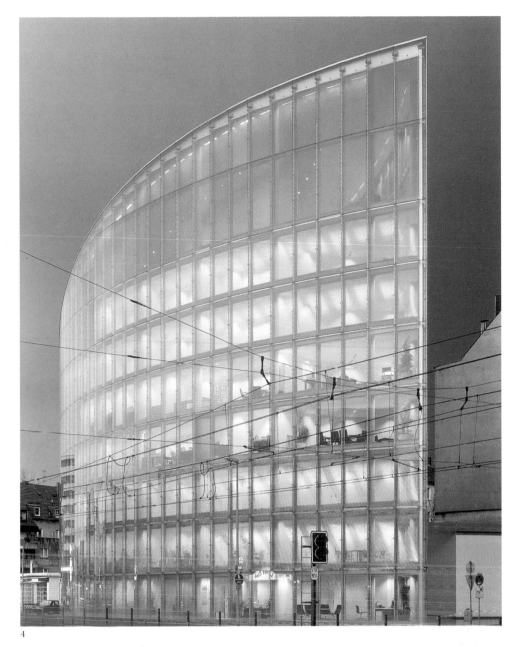

4

5

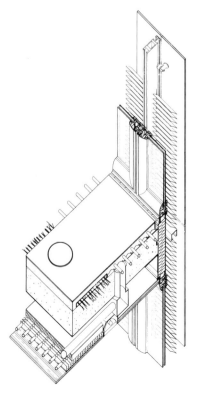

6

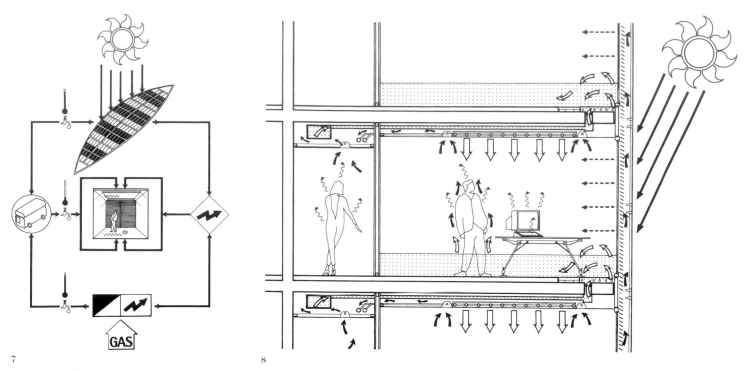

7 8

9

10

Telematic Centre

Design/Completion 1988/1993
Duisburg, Germany
GTT Kaiser Bautechnik
3,500 square metres
Concrete frame
Exposed concrete, suspended glass wall, carpet, stainless steel, stone and plasterboard

As part of the proposals for the Duisburg Micro-Electronic Park master plan, the Telematic Centre provides a focus for the development.

The building is circular in form with offices arranged round an 11-metre-wide full-height atrium. These offices house the management centre for the whole park complex as well as providing space for small and medium-sized companies moving into the neighbourhood.

The central forum at the heart of the building provides a public space for exhibitions, conferences, seminars, and musical and theatrical performances. There is also a restaurant and bar.

1

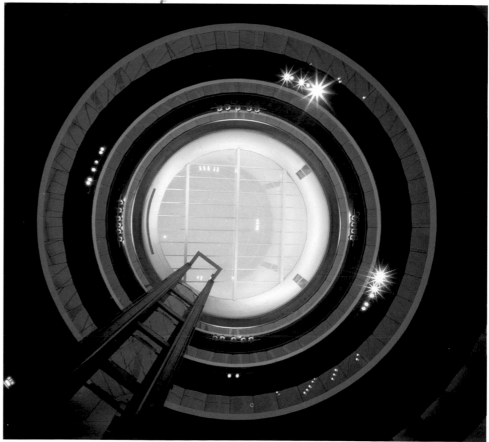

2

3

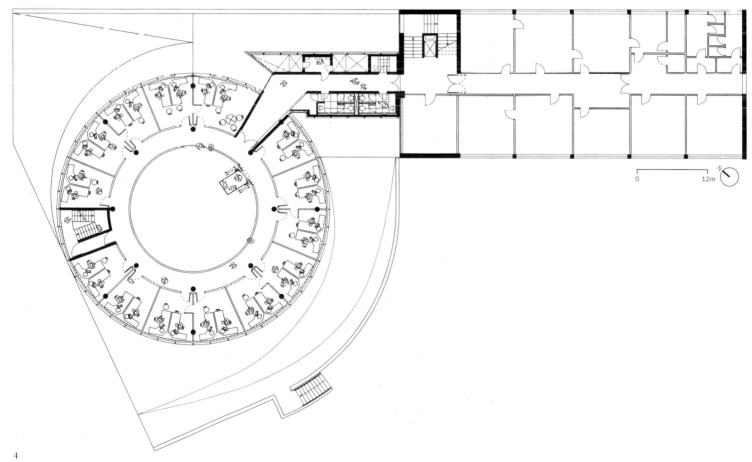

4

1   Cross-section
2   View looking up atrium
3   Exterior
4   Plan

Micro-Electronic Centre

Design/Completion 1988/1996
Duisburg, Germany
GTT
15,000 square metres
In-situ concrete frame, steel roof structure
Timber, glass, plasterboard, fabric ceiling, carpet

A master plan was established in 1988 to integrate the new, clean industries that are replacing the blighted local heavy industry, into a residential district of Duisburg in the Ruhr heartland. The master plan creates a new public park and three buildings. The first two, a Business Promotion Centre and a Telematic Centre, were completed in 1993. The largest building on the site, the Micro-Electronic Centre, was completed in 1996.

The Micro-Electronic Centre provides flexible multi-use accommodation, such as laboratories, production areas, classrooms, offices and meeting rooms, appropriate for the micro-electronics industry. The new park that links the three buildings covers half the site and will form the main circulation route between them. The views from the workspaces and the quality of daylight, as well as the air quality, are enhanced by this green space, which will also benefit the surrounding residential areas.

Within an overall climatic envelope, three fingers of accommodation are separated by two glazed atria which create a sheltered buffer zone for exhibitions and cafés. Saving energy is a key issue, and passive environmental systems are used wherever possible. The building combines external shading with natural ventilation for all offices at the perimeter. It also draws on district heating from the city's coal-fired generator.

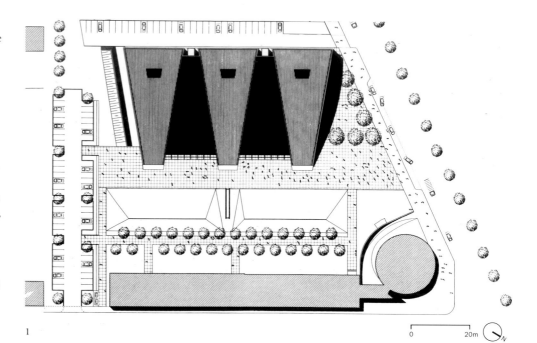

1

1 Site plan
2 Plan view of model
3 Cross-section
4 Upper level plan
5 Atrium

2

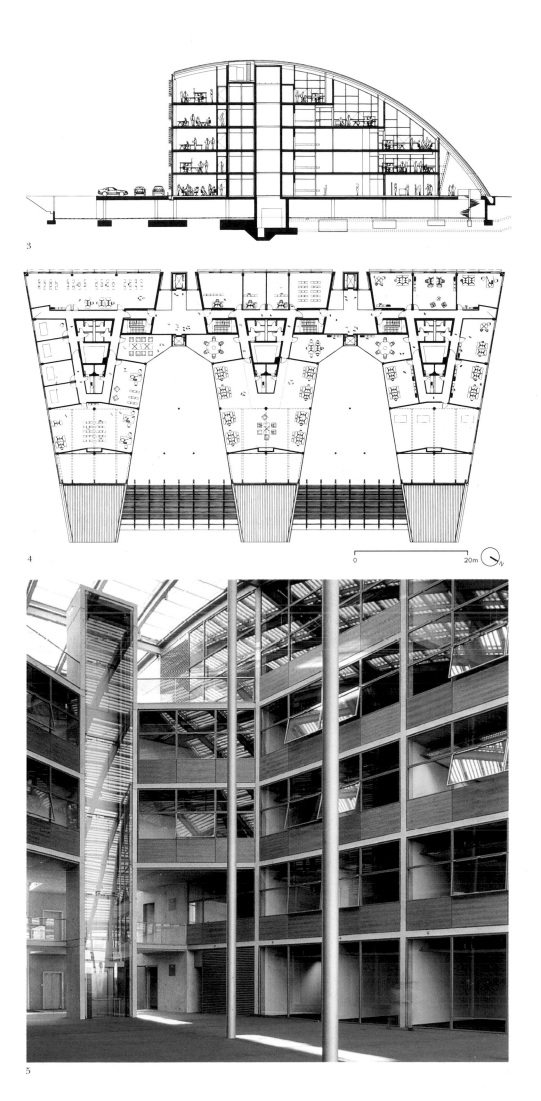

3

4

0   20m N

5

6

7

8

9

11

10

6 Night view of exterior
7 Interior
8 Exterior perimeter canopy
9 Interior
10 Rear exterior elevation
11 Interior detail

Millennium Tower

Design 1989
Tokyo, Japan
Obayashi Corporation
1,039,206 square metres
Steel and concrete clad external structure, steel reinforced
concrete internal core
Aluminium and glass

At 840 metres and 170 storeys high, the proposed Millennium Tower will be four times the height of the average Manhattan skyscraper and almost twice the height of the Sears Tower.

Rising out of Tokyo Bay, 2 kilometres offshore, the tower will be a miniature vertical township, similar in size to Tokyo's Ginza or New York's Fifth Avenue, providing hotels, shops and residential apartments as well as office space.

The building is conceived as a huge needle, bound in a helical steel cage, rising out of a marina. It will be linked to the mainland by road and rail. The primary circulation route, up the tower, will be by means of a vertical "metro" of giant lift cars capable of carrying 160 people at a time. These will stop at sky centres every 30 floors, and visitors will complete their journey by high-speed lifts.

Continued

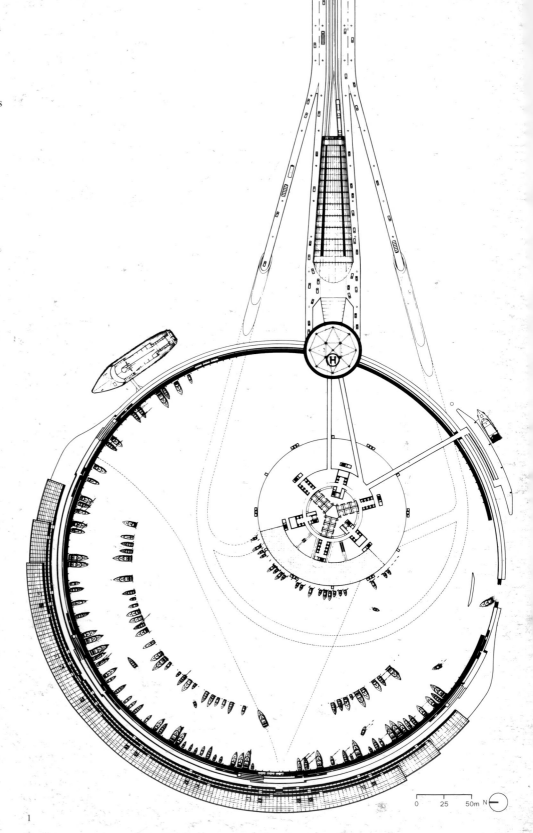

1   Site plan
Opposite:
    Artist's impression

1

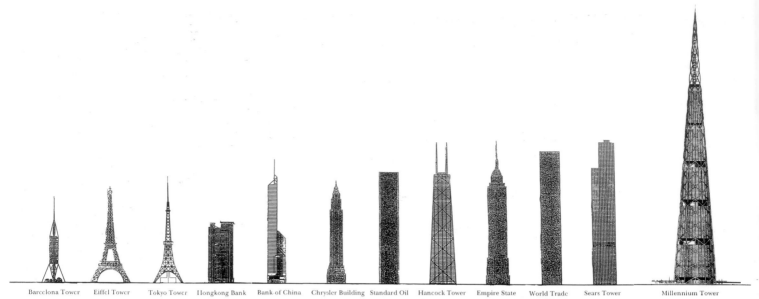

Barcelona Tower   Eiffel Tower   Tokyo Tower   Hongkong Bank   Bank of China   Chrysler Building   Standard Oil   Hancock Tower   Empire State   World Trade   Sears Tower   Millennium Tower

3

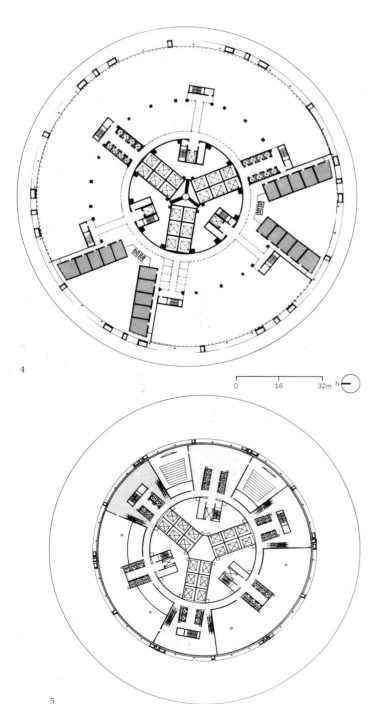

4

5

0   16   32m   N

6

3   Height comparison
4   Typical office floor, level 17
5   Sky centre B, level 61
6   Detail of model
7   Artist's impression of marina
8   Model: base of tower and marina

7

8

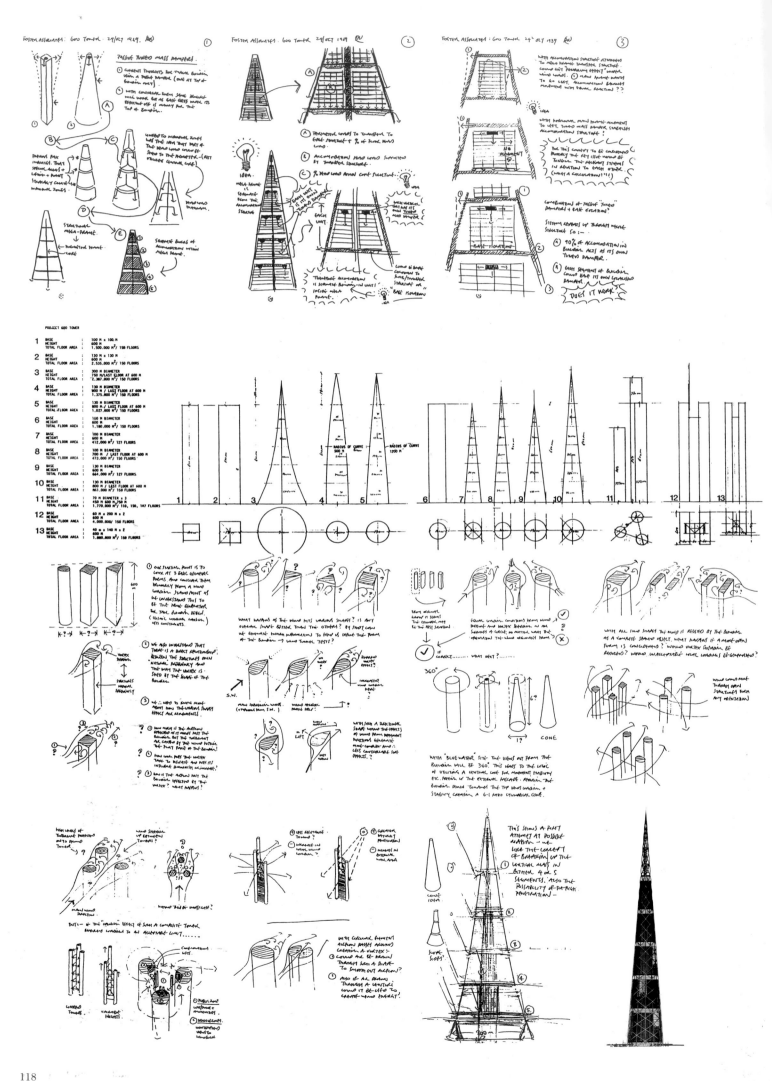

The tower is conceived as a place of work, manufacture, leisure and habitation. It offers a technological solution to human and social challenges, which are liable to become more and more pressing in the world's most densely crowded conurbations.

Opposite:
Design studies
10 Elevation view of model
11 Section and elevation

10

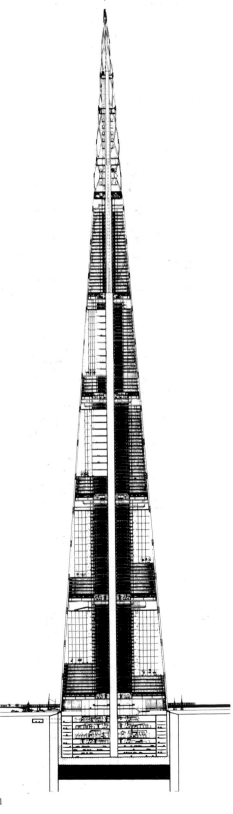

11

Cranfield University Library

Design/Completion 1989/1992
Bedfordshire, England
Cranfield University
3,000 square metres
Concrete structure, steel mullions
Concrete, steel, aluminium, slate, concrete blockwork,
polymer roof

Cranfield University is Britain's leading technical education and research establishment and a major foreign currency earner for research contracts. The new library is intended to enhance the university's standing by providing a much-needed focus and, at the same time, revising the concepts of a library in the information age. With its barrel-vaulted entrance canopy and broad central atrium, the library is the antithesis of the closed bookstore with forbidding screens and security barriers.

Perimeter desks are fitted with computer plug-in points to provide students with access to computer networks and on-line electronic databases. Seven kilometres of open book stacks have been banished to the upper level, freeing the ground floor entrance area for social uses, centred around the coffee bar. The restrained use of high-quality materials kept the cost of the new library comparable to that of a traditional brick building.

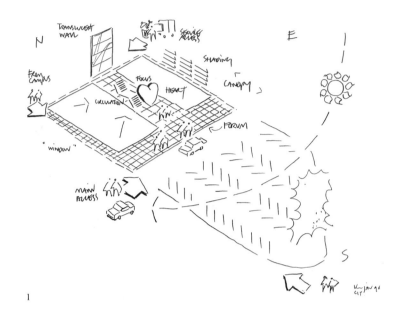

1

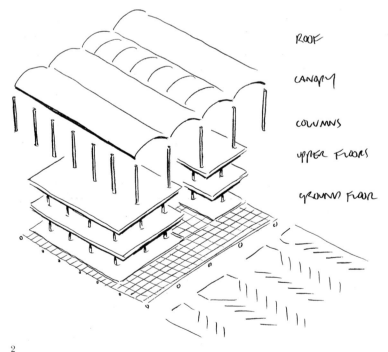

2

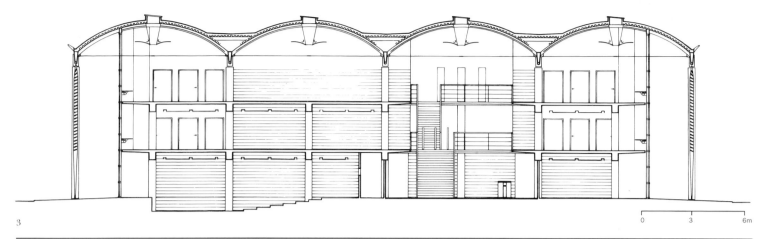

3

4

5

1&2   Sketches
3   Cross-section
4   Exterior at night
5   Entrance canopy

6

7

8

9

10

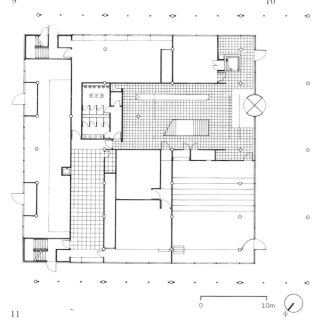

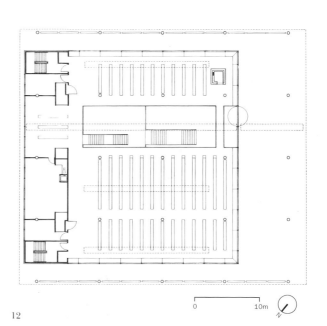

11

0   10m

12

0   10m

University of Cambridge, Faculty of Law

Competition/Completion 1990/1995
Cambridge, England
University of Cambridge
8,360 square metres
Mild steel structure
Exposed concrete, reconstituted stone, stainless steel, glass, carpet

The University of Cambridge Law Faculty building, surrounded by lawns and mature trees, sits in the heart of the Sidgwick site, the focus of arts teaching at Cambridge. The four-storey building, with a further two storeys below ground level, comprises the new Squire Law Library, five auditoria, seminar rooms, common rooms and administration offices, and is within easy reach of the Institute of Criminology and University Library. The plan is in the form of a rectangle cut on the diagonal to respond to the primary circulation on the site, the form of the Faculty of History and the fine trees on the lawn in front.

The library occupies the top three floors and enjoys uninterrupted views of the gardens through the fully glazed north-facing elevation. The ground floor contains administrative offices and the senior common room. The lower ground floors are taken up by auditoria, book stores and the student common room and are lit naturally by means of a full-height atrium and structural glass floors.

Continued

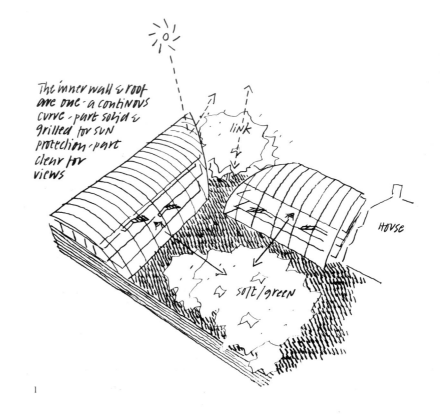

1

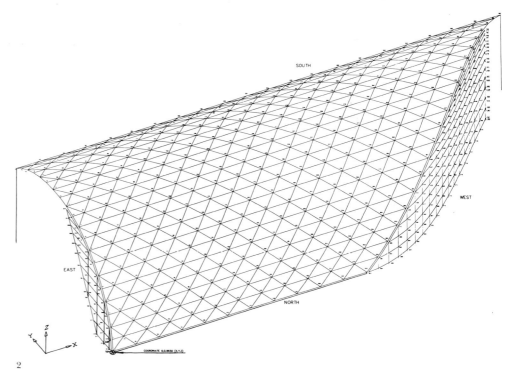

2

3

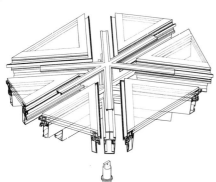

1 Concept sketch by Norman Foster
2 Axonometric of structural glazing
3 Exterior
4 Glazing detail

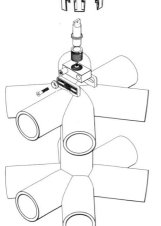

4

green wedge

phase2

phase1

entrance →

← entrance

←---- link below ground ----→

6

7

8

5 Exterior glass wall at night
6 Concept sketch by Norman Foster
7 Roof detail at entrance canopy
8 Curved glass wall

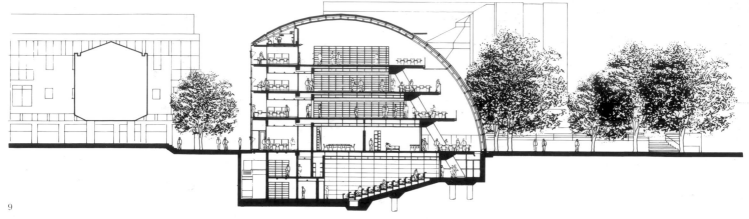

9

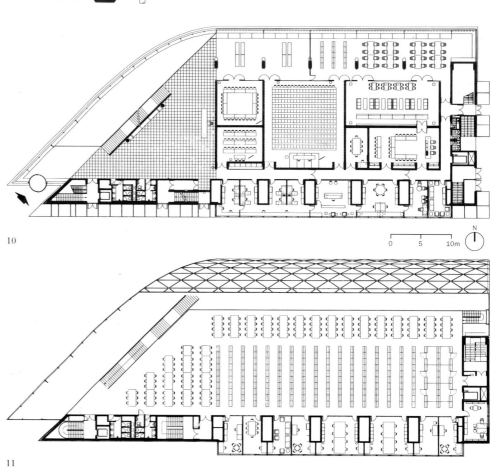

10

11

9   Cross-section
10   Ground floor plan
11   Third floor plan
12   Interior of atrium

13

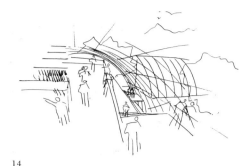

The external envelope is of high energy performance. The north facade is composed of structural silicon glazing on the same triangular grid, running in an unbroken curve into a stainless steel roof. The vertical southern elevation is clad partly in reconstituted Portland stone and partly in white glass with clear opening lights.

14

15

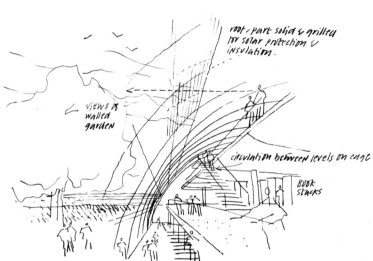

16

17

13   Interior
14   Concept sketch by Norman Foster
15   Library shelving designed by Foster and Partners
16   Concept sketch by Norman Foster
17   Interior

Lycée Albert Camus

Competition/Completion 1991/1993
Fréjus, France
Ville de Fréjus
14,500 square metres
In-situ concrete structure
Concrete, stone, glass

The school's linear plan form is a response to its site, to the social structure of the school and to a low-energy concept for the Mediterranean climate. A single linear street is bisected by the entrance space which, with its own café, acts as a meeting point for the students.

The design of the building separates the public entrance side on the north from the more private southern edge, with its magnificent views and fine trees. The two-storey classroom and double-height reception spaces within the same structure permitted economical, speedy construction and also take advantage of fine views of the sea and hills.

Materials were chosen to suit local construction techniques and the climate. The exposed concrete frame exploits the French tradition of high-quality in-situ concrete and also acts to absorb heat and thus control the rate of temperature change within the building.

Continued

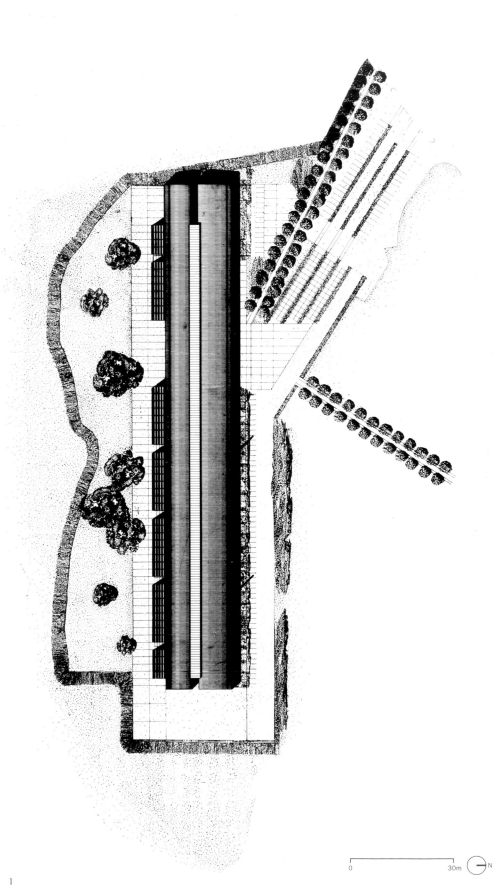

0   30m   N

1

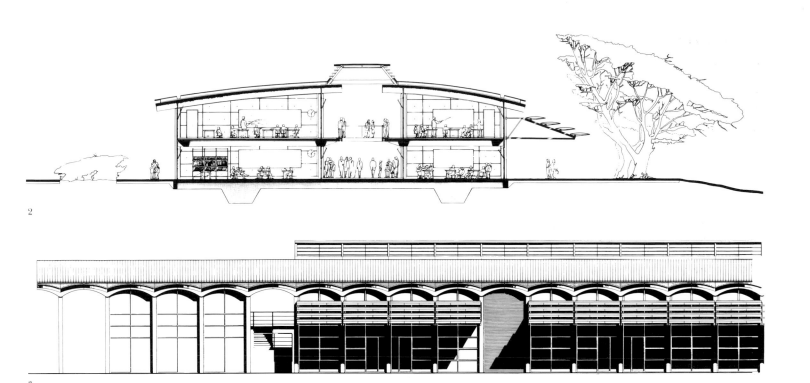

2

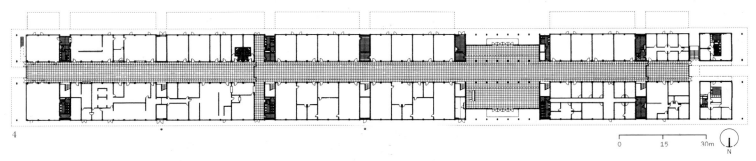

3

4

0 15 30m

N

5

1 Site plan
2 Cross-section
3 Elevation detail
4 Ground floor plan
5 Exterior

The double-height cavity between the roof and concrete vaults uses ventilation techniques of traditional Arab architecture. A solar chimney allows warm air to rise through ventilation louvres whilst a brise soleil provides a broad band of dappled shade along the southern elevation. The aim throughout was to keep active building services to a minimum. The form and construction of the building play a major part in its heating, cooling and ventilation.

6

7

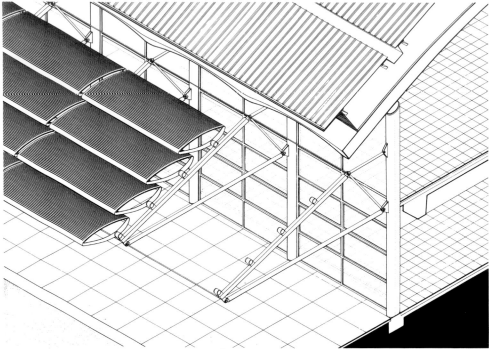

8

9

6   Exterior
7   Detail of brise soleil
8   Detail perspective of brise soleil
9&10   Exterior
11   Energy strategy
12   Arabic houses with double-skinned roofs
13   Interior

10

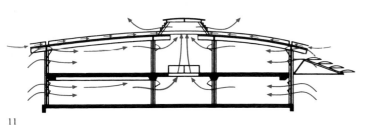

11

12

13

Inner Harbour Master Plan

Competition 1991
Duisburg, Germany
City of Duisburg Consortium/Kaiser Bautechnik/THS/LEG
89 hectares

The coal and steel town of Duisburg occupies a key geographical position between the Rhine and the Ruhr. However, the decline of the heavy steel industry, which until recently had underpinned the economy of the region, has created industrial wastelands and caused the decline of the city's large inner harbour. The priorities were to reverse urban decay and overcome unemployment levels, which in the late 1980s were running at 26 per cent of the local population.

The inner harbour is to be redeveloped as a city centre park with canals of clean water to encourage fish and plant life. An inherently flexible master plan includes new construction and the refurbishment of existing empty dockland

Continued

1 2 3

4

5

1&2   Harbour sketches by Norman Foster
   3   Model showing Eurogate building in
       master plan
   4   Section through Eurogate
   5   Model of Eurogate

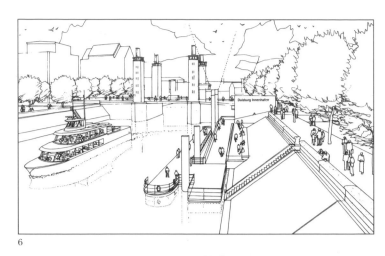

6

7

8

9

10

warehousing for residential, cultural or commercial use. All proposed solutions are intended to unify the inner city of Duisburg with the harbour area. There is also an emphasis on using passive energy systems and renewable energy sources wherever possible. The first phase of the strategy was completed in 1994 with the opening of the Steiger Schwanentor, a pleasure boat pier, and in 1996 the harbour forum offices were completed.

11

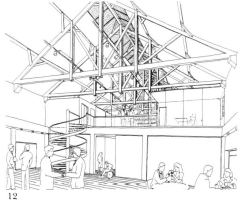

12

13

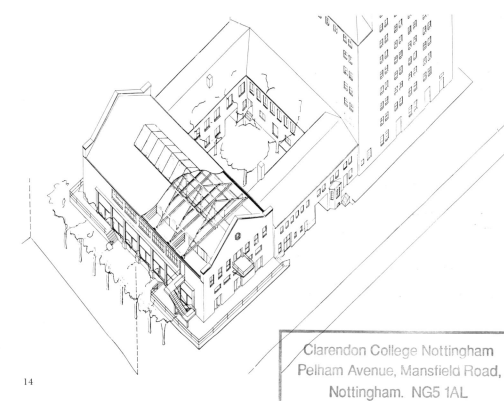

14

6 Perspective of Steiger Schwanentor
7 Detail of Steiger Schwanentor pier
8&9 Pontoon and ramps
10 View of pier from Inner Harbour
11 Interior of Hafenforum
12 Interior perspective of Hafenforum
13 Exterior of Hafenforum
14 Aerial perspective of Hafenforum

Inner Harbour Master Plan 139

Commerzbank Headquarters

Competition/Completion 1991/1997
Frankfurt, Germany
Commerzbank Ag/Nervus
100,000 square metres
Steel structure, concrete cores
Steel, concrete, glass, aluminium cladding, stone

This competition-winning scheme for the Commerzbank provided an opportunity to design a building which is symbolically and functionally "green": the world's first ecological high-rise tower. The form of the tower is triangular, made up of three "petals"—the office floors—and a central "stem"—a great central atrium which provides a natural ventilation chimney. Four-storey-high gardens spiral around the building form giving each desk a view of greenery and eliminating large expanses of unbroken office space. Every office is designed to have natural ventilation with opening windows.

Lifts, staircases and services are placed in the three corners in groups, to reinforce the village-like clusters of offices and gardens. Pairs of vertical masts, enclosing the corner cores, support eight-storey vierendeel beams, which in turn support clear span office floors.

Continued

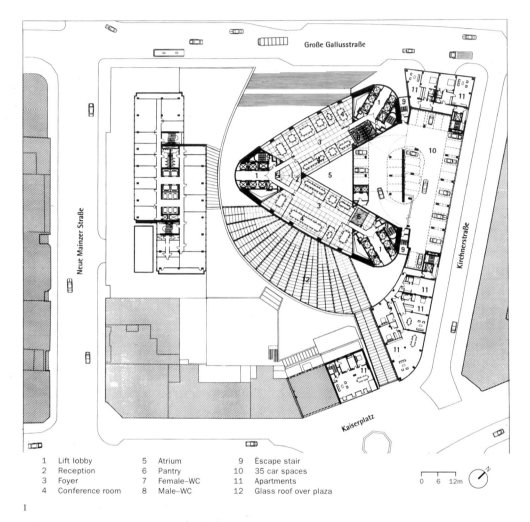

1	Lift lobby	5	Atrium	9	Escape stair
2	Reception	6	Pantry	10	35 car spaces
3	Foyer	7	Female–WC	11	Apartments
4	Conference room	8	Male–WC	12	Glass roof over plaza

1

2

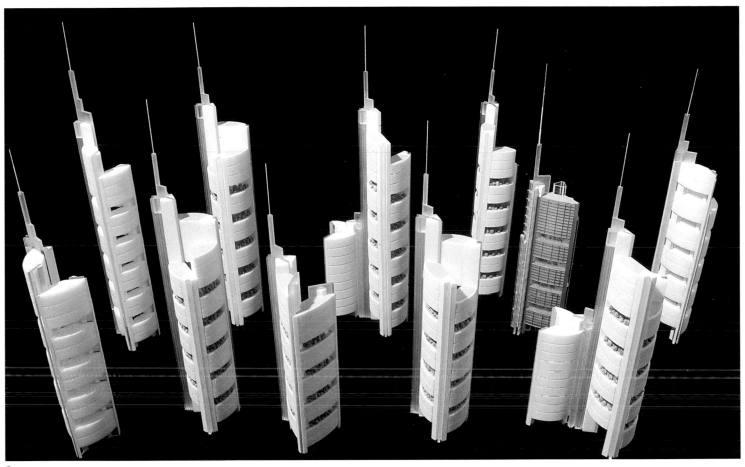

3

4

5

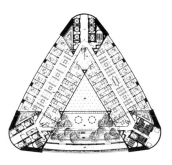

6

1   Site plan and floor plan
2   Night view
3   Models showing evolution of design
4   Photomontage
5   Plan view of model
6   Typical floor plan

7

The 53-storey tower, the tallest in Europe at just over 300 metres high, rises from the centre of the city block alongside the existing Commerzbank building. The rebuilding and restoration of the perimeter buildings which contain apartments and shops preserves the scale of the neighbourhood. The city block containing the tower is opened up with a new public space—a winter garden housing restaurants, cafés and space for performances and exhibitions

8

7&8   Model
  9   View from the river

10

11

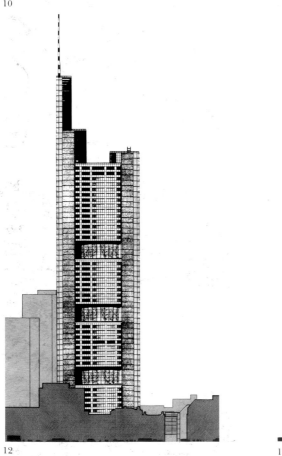

12

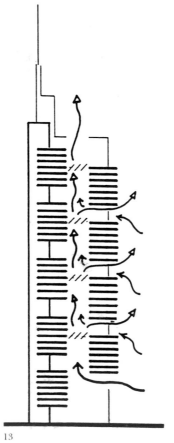

13

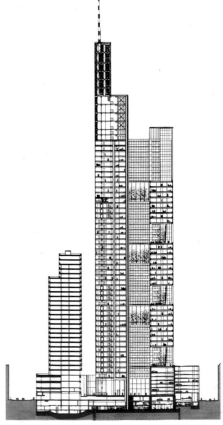

14

Motor Yacht

Design/Completion 1991/1993
Built in Bremen, Germany
Private client
Length: 60 metres
Aluminium hull and superstructure, semi-monococque
Aluminium, teak deck, timber, stainless steel

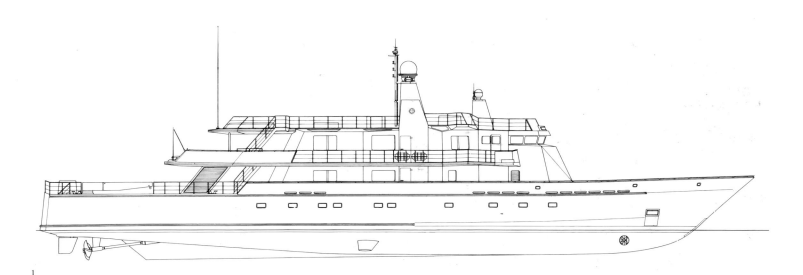

1

The design of many vessels, from floating gin palaces to cross-channel ferries, tends to split responsibilities between superstructure and hull, exterior and interior. The result is often top-heavy, unseaworthy-looking forms and interiors that are the reverse of ship-shape.

The design for this 60-metre private yacht draws inspiration from naval vessels, whose functional efficiency takes precedence over empty styling. Hull and superstructure are a semi-monococque construction of welded skin, frames and longitudinal stiffeners—the largest aluminium hull constructed to date. The interior, in keeping with the exterior, emphasises discreet, high-quality craftsmanship and appropriate materials.

2

3

1   Elevation
2   Interior
3   Exterior

Canary Wharf Station

Design/Completion 1991/1998
Canary Wharf, London
London Underground Ltd
31,500 square metres
In-situ concrete
Concrete, stainless steel, glass, stone

Canary Wharf is the largest station on the new extension to the Jubilee Line. The design seeks to minimize the physical and visual impact of above-ground station structures by creating a park above it.

Two main passenger entrances are provided in the form of large glass-domed bubbles which are illuminated at night. Each entrance spans 20 metres and is carefully integrated into the sloping grass banks at either end of the main station park which is to be Canary Wharf's principal public recreation space. A smaller third entrance is located at the eastern side of Canary Wharf to accommodate future growth.

The 300-metre-long station is of cut and cover construction, built within a reclaimed dock. Twenty escalators descend from the entrance canopies to platform level. The ticket hall is located within the station cavern together with shops, London Underground offices and public amenities. The entire cavern is clad in glass. Platform edge doors have been designed for this and all other stations on the new line.

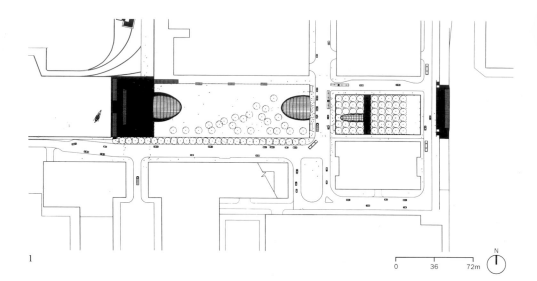

1

0   36   72m

2

3

4

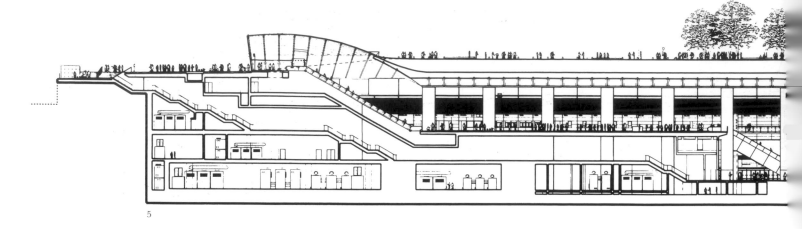

5

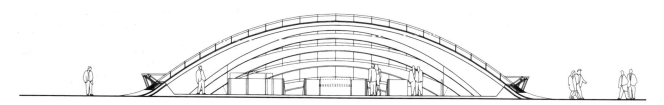

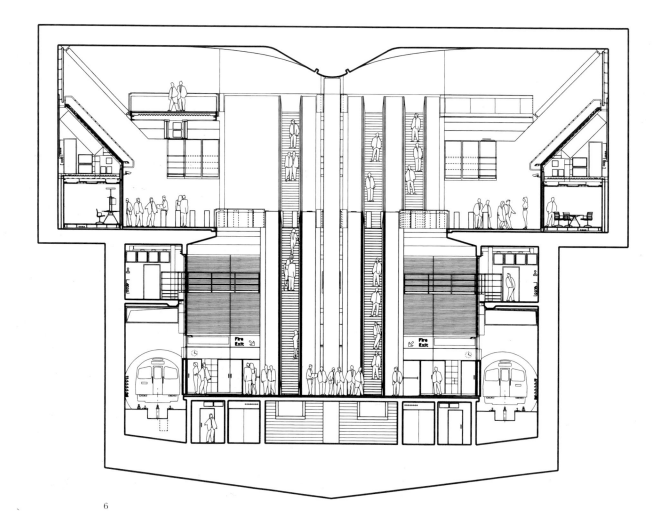

6

5 Long section
6 Cross-section
7 Ticket hall and platform level plans
8 Section model of station interior

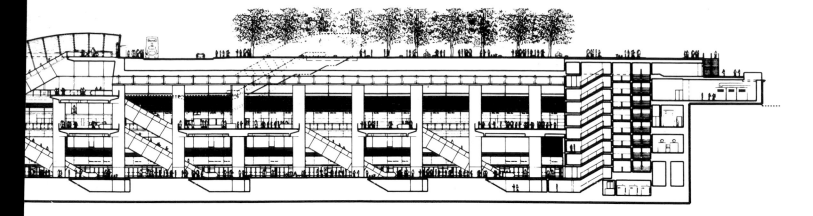

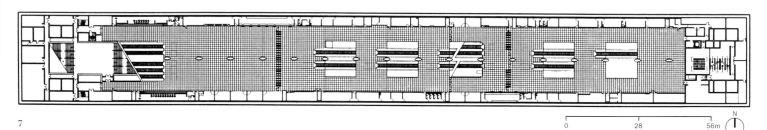

7

0　　　　28　　　　56m　N

8

Airport at Chek Lap Kok

Competition/Completion 1992/1998
Hong Kong
Airport Authority Hong Kong
515,000 square metres
Concrete superstructure, concrete columns supporting
prefabricated steel roof
Steel, concrete, glass, granite, stainless steel, aluminium

The first phase of Hong Kong's new
airport, scheduled for completion in 1998,
will create the largest airport in the world.
By 2040 the airport is expected to handle
87 million passengers a year, equivalent to
the present capacities of Heathrow and
JFK combined.

The airport is being constructed at Chek
Lap Kok, a largely man-made purpose-
built island 6 kilometres long and
3.5 kilometres wide. The terminal will be
1.5 kilometres long and the baggage hall
alone will be the size of Wembley Stadium.
Within the terminal, arriving and
departing passengers are separated by
level; clarity of movement is established by
keeping all land-side connections to the
east and air-side connections to the west.

All passengers enter and leave the
building through a vast entrance hall
atrium. The meeting and greeting area for
arrivals is on the ground level, while
departing passengers pass overhead on
glass bridges. From check-in, departing

Continued

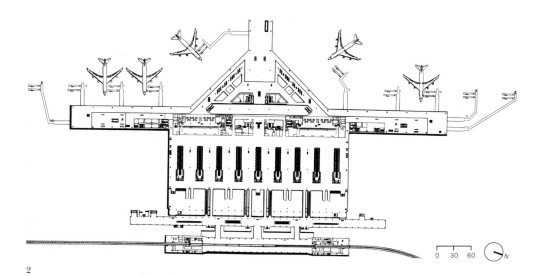

1

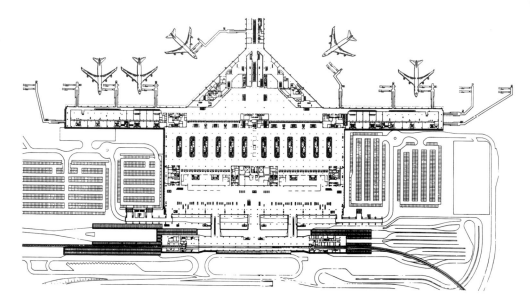

2

1   Arrivals level plan
2   Departures level plan
3   Aerial view of terminal building
4   Cross-section

3

4

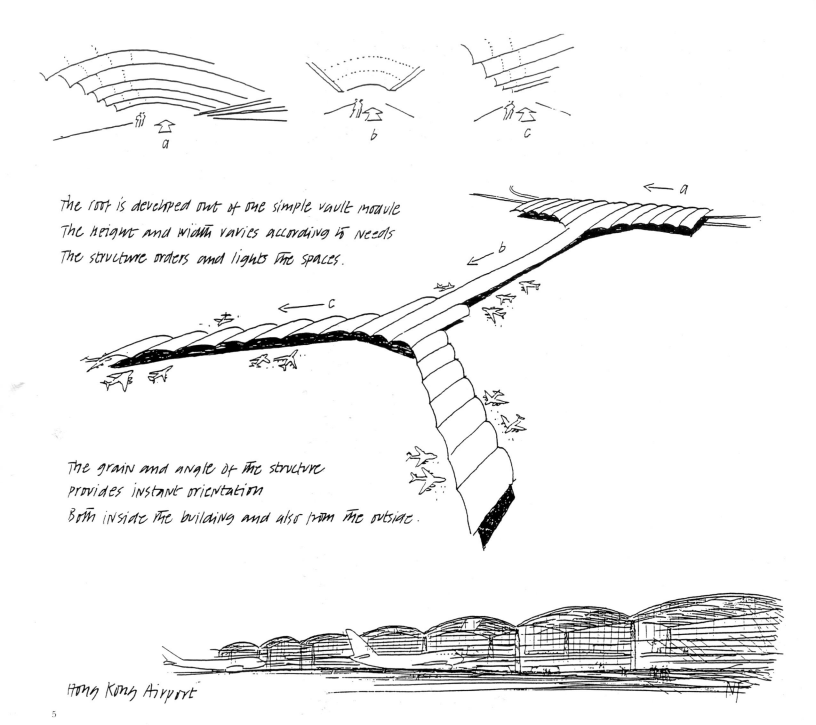

The roof is developed out of one simple vault module
The height and width varies according to needs
The structure orders and lights the spaces.

The grain and angle of the structure
provides instant orientation
Both inside the building and also from the outside.

Hong Kong Airport

5

5   Concept sketches by Norman Foster
6   Lifting of roof module

passengers pass through immigration and security control to a long, Y-shaped concourse from which all gates can be accessed by foot, moving walkway or internal train.

The concrete structure supports a series of 36-metre lightweight steel shells connected to form continuous barrel vaults running east–west, giving direction to passenger flows. The roof covers the building like a blanket, hugging its contours and unifying its various functions, while also providing the symbolic identity of the building.

6

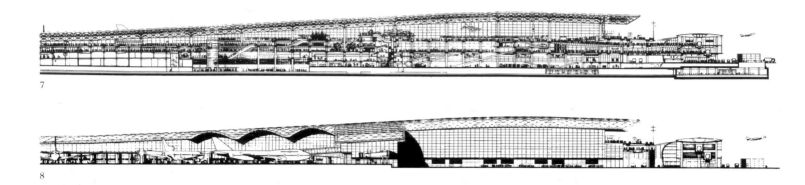

7

8

9

7 Long section
8 South elevation
9 View of terminal building at night

Kowloon Canton Railway Terminal

Design/Completion 1992/1998
Hong Kong
Kowloon Canton Railway Corporation
45,000 square metres
Steel structure
Steel, granite, glass

The original Kowloon Railway Station was built in the mid-1970s; however, the popularity and growth of this railway link to China has outstripped all expectations for daily commuters, tourists and business travellers alike. The challenge was to renovate and enlarge the station to meet this demand and to cope with the introduction of new double-decker trains to mainland China.

The existing station is divided into three levels: tracks at the lowest road and pavement level, public walkways at mid-level, and a congested concourse on a raised podium. The concourse area will be enlarged and greatly simplified into three distinct air-conditioned zones: international departures, international arrivals and domestic passengers. Each zone will be served by shops, restaurants and seating of a standard usually found only in international airports. The daily commuters will use the mid-level walkway.

The station will be expanded eastwards with a new lightweight pavilion which has a wave-like structure, doubling the size of the existing concourse. All levels will be connected by lifts and staircases in atrium voids; natural light will penetrate all parts of the building.

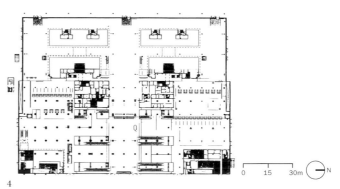

1   North–south section
2   Detail of roof structure
3   Interior of terminal
4   Concourse plan

House in Germany

Design/Completion 1992/1994
Germany
Private client
750 square metres
Concrete and steel structure
Fairface concrete, stainless steel, glass, aluminium

This private house for a young German family is built on a south-facing site with uninterrupted valley views. The site falls 18 metres below street level, so the roof terrace, with space for four parked cars, becomes the arrival level from the street. Above the terrace, a partially glazed steel structure provides covered access to the main entrance and the two side entrances to the east and west. From this level, a ramp leads down through the levels of the house to the lower garden terrace.

At lower garden level, the house opens out towards the south with living areas, bedrooms and dining areas overlooking the garden. The main living area is the family domain containing the book-lined hearth and the open kitchen on either side of a double-height living space. The owner has a special interest in cooking, which is reflected in the professionally equipped kitchen with efficient extraction system.

The upper level includes a housekeeper's flat, four children's bedrooms and a small library. The southern facade is completely glazed with alternating transparent and translucent panels to vary the quality of light and degree of privacy.

The unusual combination of inside and outside circulation enables the house to offer family members and their friends an exceptional degree of community, as well as respecting their privacy.

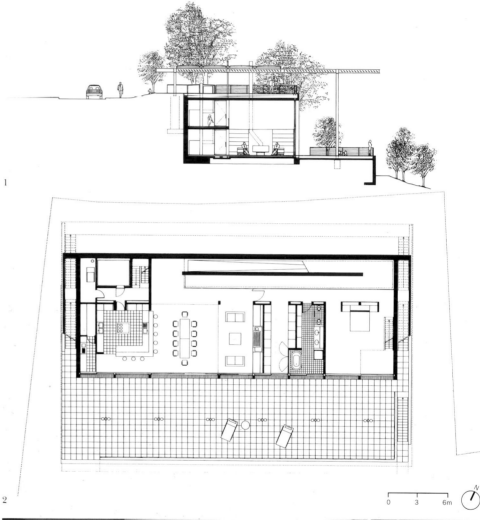

1

2

0   3   6m

1   Cross-section through living area
2   Lower level plan
3   Interior
4   Garden elevation
5   Entrance ramp from upper level
6   Exterior

3

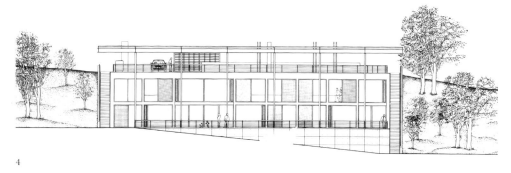

4

5

6

Musée de la Préhistoire, Verdon

Design 1992
Quinson, Gorges du Verdon, France
Département Alpes de Haute-Provence
4,274 square metres
Concrete structure
Precast concrete, stone, timber

The form of the building is directly inspired by the rugged landscape that surrounds the site; it is a positive and deliberately precise incision into that landscape. The contours of the adjacent ground are therefore adjusted until the two-storey building appears to be almost completely buried.

Internally, the museum is organized on two levels, with a vast, top-lit, elliptical space at ground level. This internal hall forms a focus for reception, restaurant and public information functions. The private spaces for research and administration and the workshops are also at this level, though separated behind glass screens. The route to the museum from the hall is by a long ramp, which begins in the central space and follows the curved line of the high stone wall until it reaches the mezzanine level.

The museographic spaces have been designed to be completely flexible and able to accommodate any current or future reorganization.

The design of the museum is one of totally integrated public and private areas gathered around a major space. Natural light is exploited in the main circulation areas, but is limited in the exhibition rooms where it is not required.

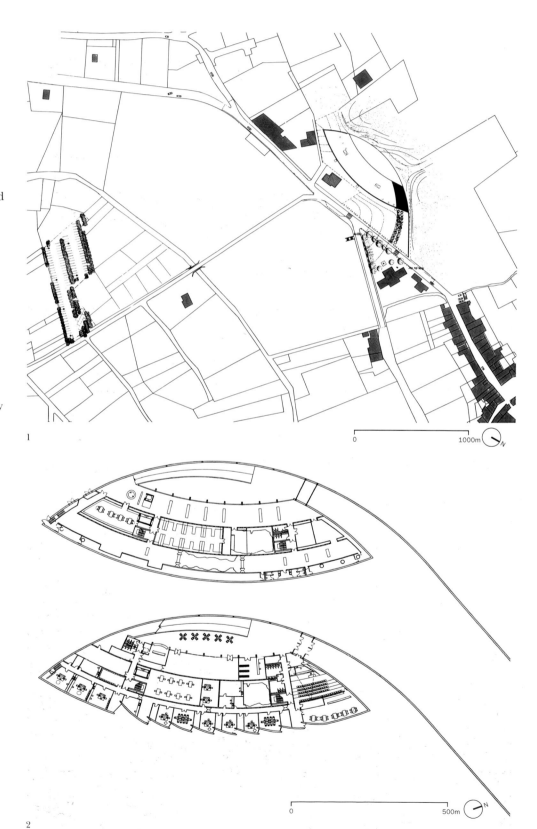

1 Site plan
2 First floor and ground floor plans
3 Elevation of museum
4 Section
5 CAD view of exterior
6 CAD view of interior

3

4

5

6

Solar Electric Vehicle

Design/Completion 1992/1994
Kew Gardens, London, England
Robert and Lisa Sainsbury Charitable Trust/Royal Botanic Gardens, Kew
Dimensions: 7.2 metres long, 2.5 metres high, 2.3 metres wide
Mild steel RHS hoop structure to superstructure, mild steel RHS chassis
Glass fibre-reinforced polyester and foam composite panel construction, curved laminated safety glass

Alternative forms of transport are often explored within environments such as parks, well away from the pollution and anarchy of the public highway. This prototype electric vehicle stemmed from a project for the Royal Botanic Gardens at Kew. Its sponsors, Sir Robert and Lady Sainsbury, had been much impressed by the miniature train at Versailles and proposed something similar for the benefit of visitors to Kew Gardens.

The vehicle is based on a modified standard diesel chassis with a superstructure of mild steel hoops and glass-reinforced polyester body panels. The side glazing carries up over the roof in a single panel to enhance a feeling of transparency. An air cushion suspension on all four wheels allows the cabin level to be lowered almost flush with the ground, for the benefit of disabled users. The vehicle is powered both by batteries and by photovoltaic cells mounted on the roof, and has a top speed of 24 km/h.

We are currently developing a gas turbine hybrid with Imperial College to achieve a cruising speed of 50 km/h and a maximum speed of 110 km/h.

1

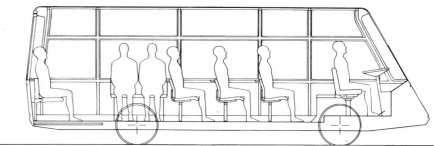

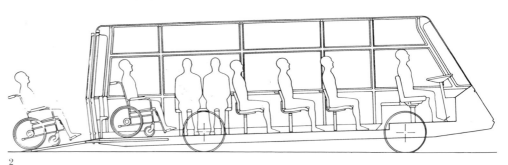

2

3

4

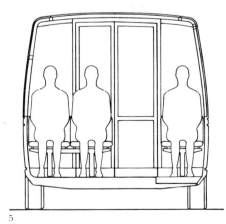

5

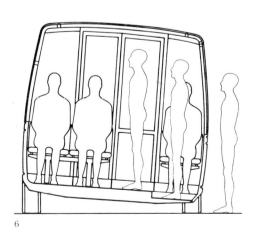

6

1 Exterior
2 Long section
3 Interior
4 Exterior showing wheelchair access
5 Cross-section showing seating
6 Cross-section showing loading

New German Parliament, Reichstag

Design/Completion 1992/1999
Berlin, Germany
Federal Republic of Germany (Bündesbaugesellschaft Berlin mbH)
61,166 square metres
Existing building masonry with new steel and reinforced concrete structure
Steel, concrete, glass, stone, aluminium, photovoltaic roof cladding

The initial brief for the competition was for 34,000 square metres of space, most of which was housed in a new podium wrapped around the old Reichstag. The podium responded to a traditional need to cater for large outdoor gatherings by creating an outdoor forum, with columns supporting a roof umbrella which tied together the old and the new. This roof had a symbolic importance, but it also worked ecologically by harvesting energy and aiding a system of natural ventilation.

The second stage competition asked for significantly less space, so it was necessary to start the design process again. The new proposals are rooted in four major issues: the workings of Parliament, the history of the Reichstag, ecology/energy-efficiency, and the economics of realizing the project.

Public areas become a vital part of the revised brief and in this new approach the roof becomes a major public space. Much of the existing 1960s interior will be removed and the original principal raised entrance level will be reinstated as the grand ceremonial entrance.

Continued

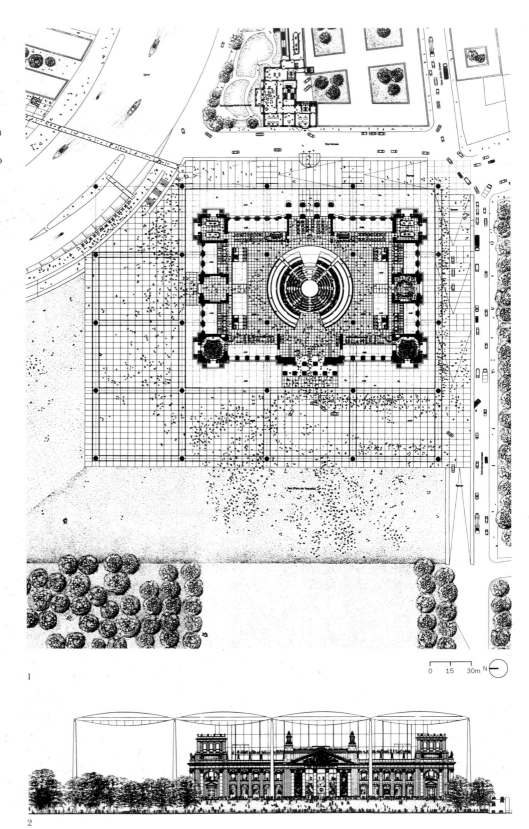

1

0   15   30m   N

2

162

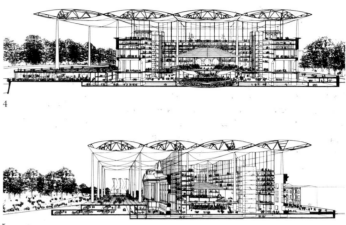

4

3

5

6

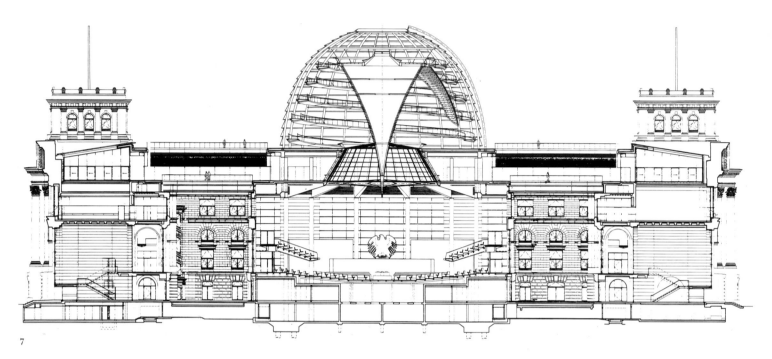

7

In peeling away the building fabric, traces of the past—such as shell marks, charred timber and the graffiti of the Russian occupation—have been revealed, and these will be preserved.

Extensive use of natural ventilation and light is proposed, combined with sophisticated systems of energy cogeneration and heat recovery. The final design incorporates a roof structure or cupola, which will deflect controlled daylight into the Plenary Chamber below and also scoop out air as part of the natural ventilation system. The structure will also contain an array of photovoltaic cells as a part of the energy system and provide support for an elevated viewing deck with access by helical ramps.

8

7   Section through final scheme
8   Models showing evolution of dome design
9   Norman Foster sketch of dome
10   Model of final scheme
11&12   Model of dome

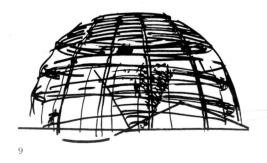

9

10

11

12

13

14

15

16

17

13 Photomontage
14 Dome mock-up being erected on roof of Reichstag
15 Dome mock-up on the roof of Reichstag
16 Photomontage of final design scheme
17 Construction of the Plenary Chamber
18 Construction progress: the main entrance being propped up

18

Addition to Joslyn Art Museum

Competition/Completion 1992/1994
Omaha, Nebraska, USA
Joslyn Art Museum
5,800 square metres
Steel structure
Marble-clad precast concrete external wall, stone floors,
timber block floor, plasterboard

Built in 1931, the Joslyn Art Museum
in Omaha, Nebraska, is one of the finest
Art Deco buildings in America. It houses
a 1,200-seat concert hall flanked by art
galleries.

The brief called for 5,000 square metres
of extra gallery and workshop space, as
well as some limited refurbishment of the
existing building. The challenge was to
re-emphasise the underused majestic
public front of the museum and design
a new wing which did not detract from
the simplicity of the original building.
The new wing is a solid rectangular form,
with little articulation but similar
proportions to the existing museum.

The addition is clad in matching pink
marble from the same quarry that
supplied the original building materials
in the 1930s. Linking new and old, and
set back from both, is a glass atrium,
providing restaurant space and
a secondary public entrance. The main
level of the new wing contains temporary
Continued

1

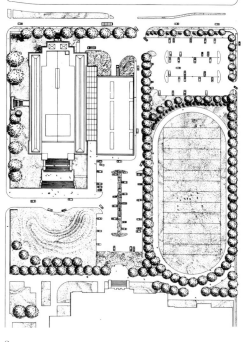

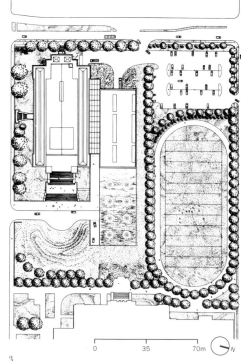

2

3

0   35   70m

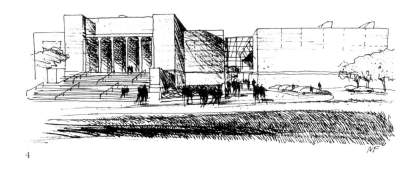

4

5

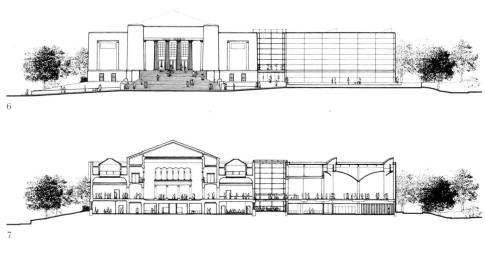

6

7

1 Gallery exterior
2 Site plan, phase I
3 Proposed site plan, phase II
4 Norman Foster sketch
5 Entrance to connecting atrium at night
6 East elevation
7 Cross-section

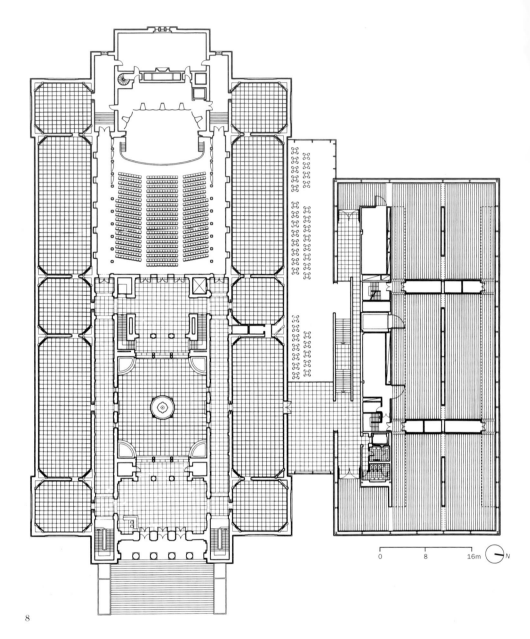

8

9

10

exhibition space, lit from above by indirect, controllable daylight. Beneath are storage vaults, workshops, cloakrooms and a new kitchen and servery for the restaurant.

The contract was completed on time and 5 per cent below budget, allowing additional restoration work to be carried out on the original building.

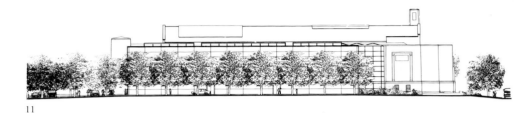

11

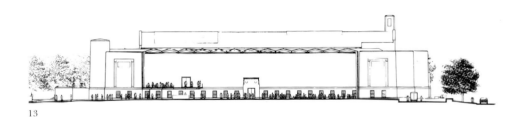

12

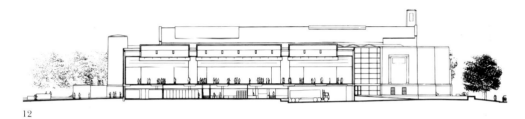

13

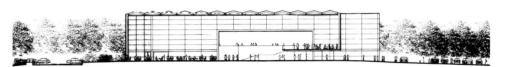

14

15

16

Congress Centre, Valencia

Design/Completion 1993/1998
Valencia, Spain
City of Valencia
16,000 square metres
Concrete frame, precast composite and in-situ concrete roof
Fairface concrete, limestone, glass, zinc, aluminium, steel, granite

The Valencia Congress Centre will be one of the leading conference centres in Europe. Located to the north-east of the city on a new urban block which contains a park, mixed-use buildings and a hotel, the centre will act as a gateway to the city and a marker for the new urban area of Ademuz Polygon.

There are to be three auditoria, providing seating for 1,500, 500 and 250 people respectively. A multi-use room for 250 is included, together with a restaurant, a café/bar and banqueting room, administrative offices, and retail and support areas. The design of the building blends exterior and interior in its use of translucent stone, which provides an additional veil for the interior while preventing excessive heat gain.

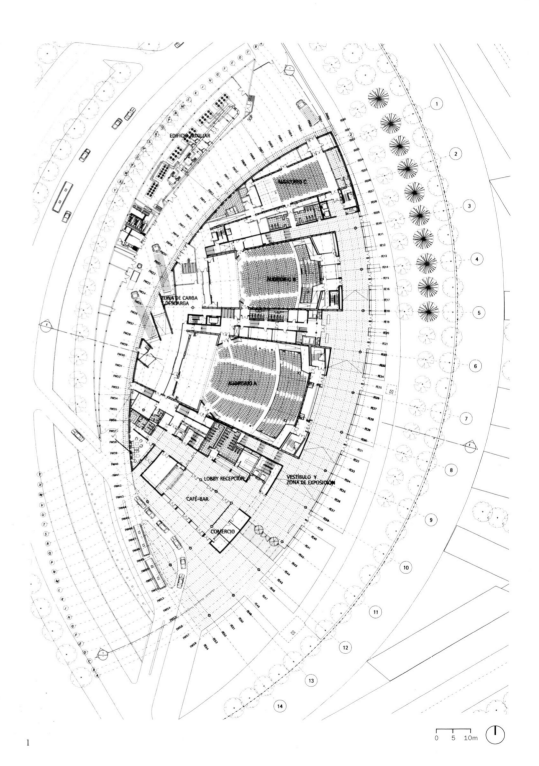

1

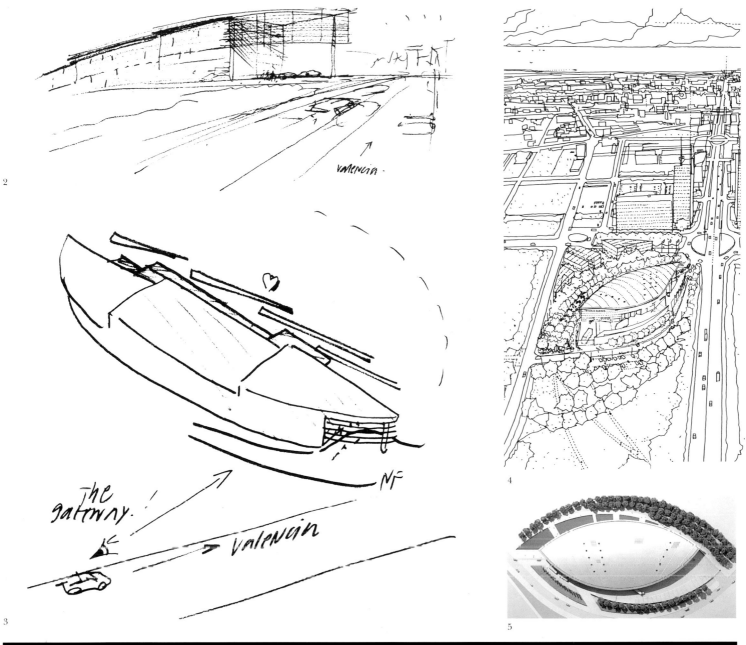

1   Ground level plan
2&3   Norman Foster concept sketches
4   Aerial perspective
5   Plan view of model
6   Model

7

8

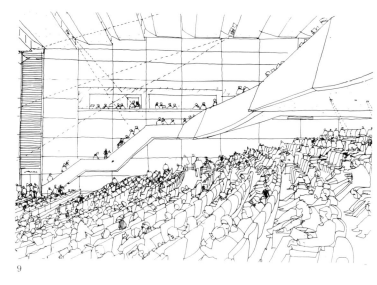

9

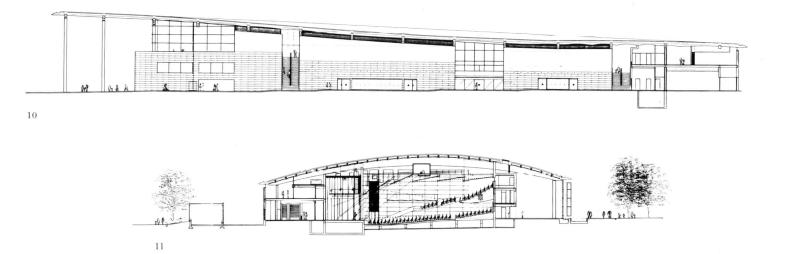

10

11

12

13

Offices for Electricité de France

Design/Completion 1992/1996
Bordeaux, France
Electricité de France
7,000 square metres
Concrete trough slab structure
Concrete, high-performance glass, aluminium, cedar, stone

Electricité de France wanted to gather all their various departments, previously scattered around Bordeaux, into one building. The brief called for a headquarters building with high-quality cellular office space that would embrace energy efficiency, especially in the use of electricity. The building's energy consumption is approximately half that of similar buildings in France.

The design of the landscaping responds to both the geometry of the nearby Château Raba and the warm climate of Bordeaux, with a long avenue of trees providing a majestic, sheltered entrance to the building.

The thermal mass of the exposed concrete soffits in the building helps to maintain comfortable interior temperatures during the day in the summer months. At night the windows on the east and west elevations open automatically, allowing air in to cool the concrete slabs.

Continued

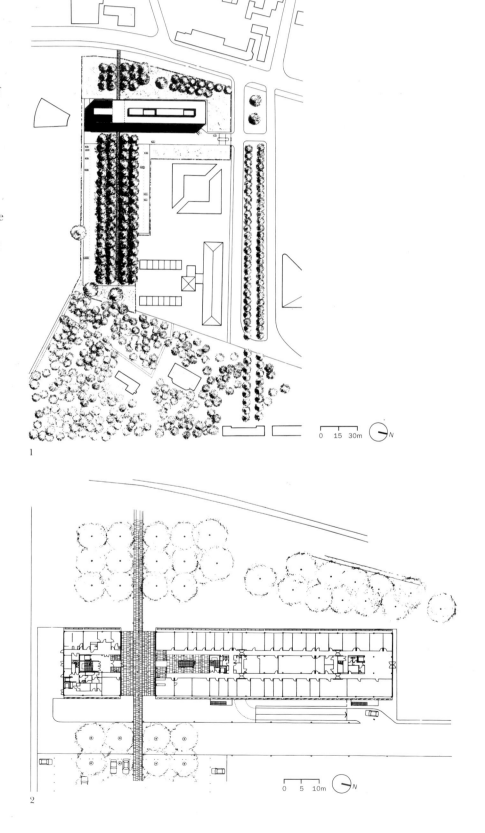

1

0 15 30m N

2

0 5 10m N

3

4

1   Site plan
2   Ground floor plan
3   Exterior
4   External louvres

Additional temperature control is provided through the floors, which can be cooled in summer and heated in winter. To prevent the building overheating, the elevations are fitted with fixed sunshades of untreated cedarwood. These provide shade at the same time as preserving views from the building.

5.

6

7

5   Exterior
6   External louvres
7   Exterior walkway
Opposite:
    Exterior walkway

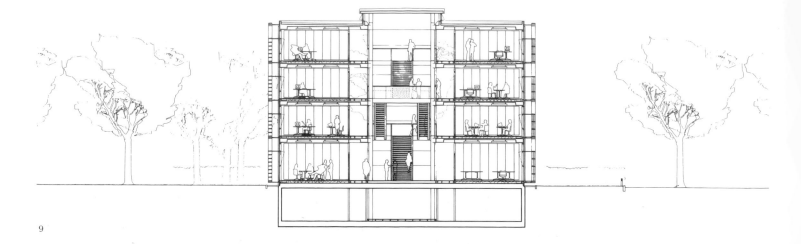

9

10

11

12

9 Cross-section
10&11 Interior stairs
12 Office interior

Millau Bridge

Competition 1993
Millau, France
Department of Transport and Public Works of France
2.5 kilometres long
Steel and concrete

1

The 2.5-kilometre-long viaduct, which will form part of the new A75 motorway between Clermont-Ferrand and Beziers, will cross the Tarn valley to the west of Millau in the Aveyron.

The new viaduct will be of epic proportions. The columns range in height from 75 to 235 metres, with the mast structures rising a further 90 metres above the road deck. In one place over the River Tarn the road deck will be 275 metres above the water.

The proposed design is a multi-span cable-stayed structure in seven sections, each section spanning 350 metres. The form of the columns is a direct response to the way a structure of this size behaves; for example, the columns need to accommodate the enormous expansion and contraction of the concrete deck. Each column therefore splits into two thinner and more flexible columns below the road deck. The cables are connected to A-frame masts in a fan arrangement between the carriageways.

The resulting form creates a dramatic silhouette against the sky—an elegant and taut structure spanning effortlessly across the valley.

2

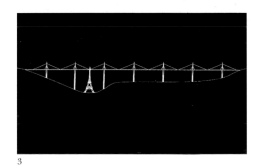

3

1&2   Photomontage views over the Tarn valley
3   Height comparison with Eiffel Tower

Al Faisaliah Complex

Competition 1993
Riyadh, Saudi Arabia
King Faisal Foundation
214,526 square metres
Concrete structure
Precast concrete cladding to low-rise, aluminium cladding to tower, granite/marble, heat mirror glass, carpet, metal ceilings, timber

This complex is a mixed-use development encompassing an office tower, a five-star luxury hotel, apartments, a retail mall and a banquet hall.

The office tower rises more than 250 metres in height and is square in plan, tapering to a point at the top in one giant arc. It is designed around a compact central core with four main corner columns defining its unique silhouette. At stages up the building, observation decks are highlighted by giant K-braces which define the structure and tie the corner columns together. Cantilevered sun-shading devices on the facade will minimize glare and allow the use of non-reflective, energy-efficient glass.

A vast banquet hall, designed to accommodate up to 1,200 guests, has been sunk below the landscaped plaza. An extraordinary degree of flexibility will be achieved by a unique long-span arch system, allowing a column-free space of 57 by 81 metres.

On opposite sides of the plaza lie the hotel and apartment buildings. These buildings have been designed using solid indigenous materials—high-quality precast concrete, local limestone and wood—to create a multi-layered facade.

The 40,000-square-metre retail mall flanking the central complex will have a 250-metre-long central atrium punctuated with controlled natural lighting and a sophisticated projector/lighting display at night. The development is anchored at each end by a two-floor department store, a food court and an entertainment centre.

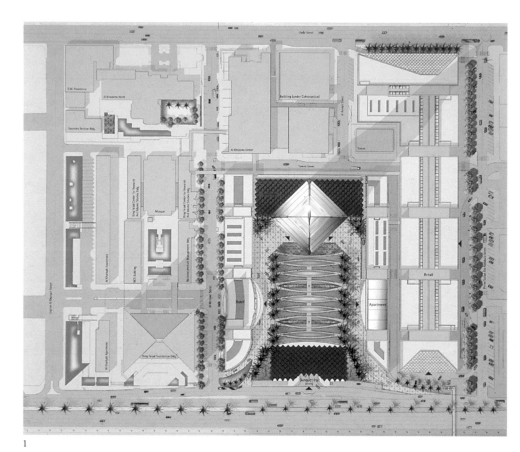

1

2

1   Site plan
2   Interior model view
3   Model view

3

Forth Valley Community Village

Design/Completion 1993/1995
Forth Valley, Scotland
Central Scotland Healthcare NHS Trust
1,500 square metres
Concrete block wall, timber frame windows, gluelam beams, standing seam aluminium roof
Concrete block, aluminium, timber, carpet, glass

1

The mentally ill need constant care and attention but in most respects their needs are not very different from those of the rest of the community. If asked what they would expect from a residential development, most people would list a degree of privacy, a sense of community, a feeling of enclosure and easy access to nature.

These are some of the features of the first phase of the Forth Valley Healthcare community care village for 42 long-term mentally ill patients. The scheme is planned as a crescent of seven houses, each accommodating six people, in the grounds of Bellsdyke Hospital. Visitors to the residences approach along a curved drive through a tree-lined meadow, as if in a country estate.

The houses have extensive glazed facades overlooking a "village green" at the centre of the crescent and each house has a different climbing plant on its entrance wall. At the heart of the scheme is a large living/dining and kitchen area, with a vaulted ceiling admitting top lighting. The curved form of the building, both in plan and section, and its intimate scale, have been used here in a deliberate attempt at avoiding hard, aggressive forms.

2

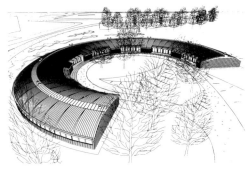

3

1&2 Exterior
  3 CAD perspective
  4 Site plan
  6 Interior

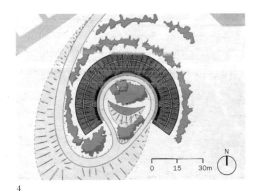

4

5

Telecommunications Facility

Design 1994
Santiago de Compostela, Spain
Concello de Santiago de Compostela
4,100 square metres
Steel structure, steel superstructure
Steel, composite steel and concrete slabs, aluminium roof, glass cladding, sandwich panel cladding, aluminium cladding panels

The aim of the project was to unify all technical users within a single structure in this sensitive landscape and, at the same time, cut energy consumption and increase access by the public. The design had to be integrated into the city's master plan for the area which included a programme of reafforestation. Since there was no need to build higher than 25 metres, the design is for a horizontal platform, rather than a tall tower.

All users have independent installations on the platform, with direct access to the antennae and the twin masts. The public enter the building in glazed lifts which rise through the underside of the platform to a viewing gallery. This leads to a walkway with spectacular views over the surrounding landscape and the city centre at the base of the hill.

Continued

1

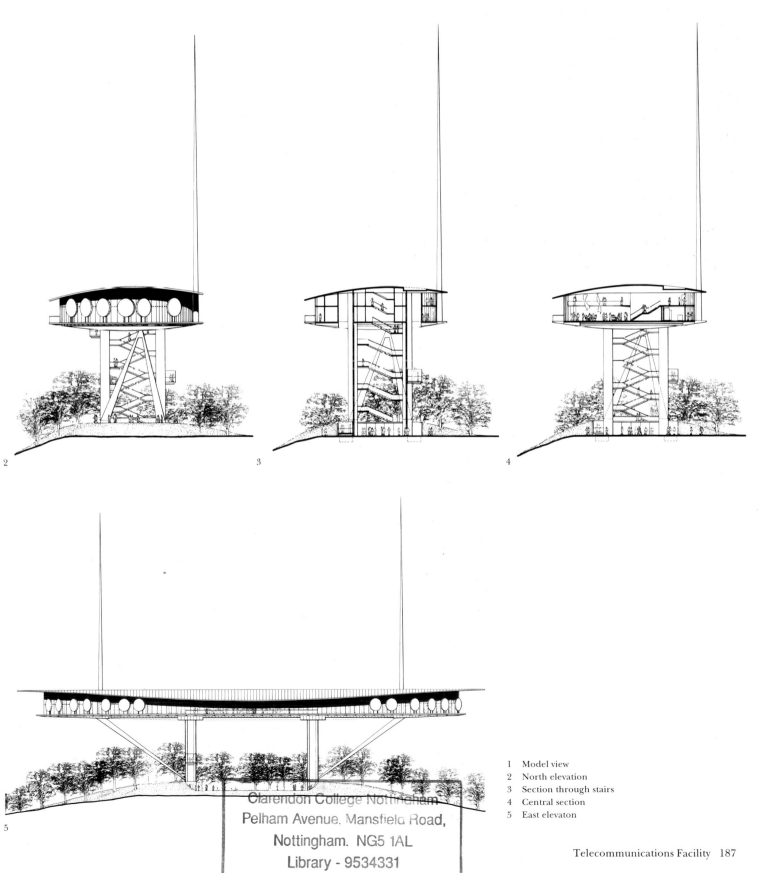

2

3

4

5

1 Model view
2 North elevation
3 Section through stairs
4 Central section
5 East elevaton

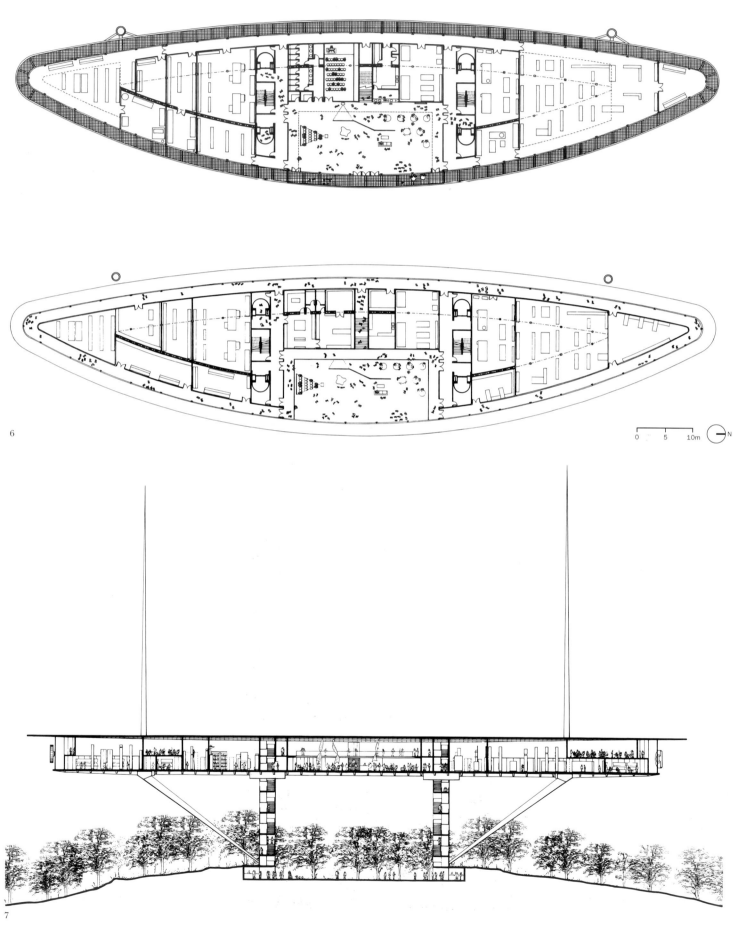

6

0   5   10m   N

7

With continuing rapid developments being made in telecommunications, the only constant is the need to adapt to change. The platform proposed for Santiago has been designed to provide maximum flexibility between public and technical use, thus helping to ensure that the building never becomes obsolete. It will also become a majestic symbol for the city, rather than an "unsightly but necessary" piece of engineering blight.

8

9

6   Plans
7   Long section
8   Model view
9   Photomontage from city

The Great Court, British Museum

Design/Completion 1994/2000
London, England
British Museum Development Trust
19,000 square metres
Lightweight steel and glass roof, in-situ concrete mezzanines and basement
Portland stone, limestone, glass, timber, paper maché

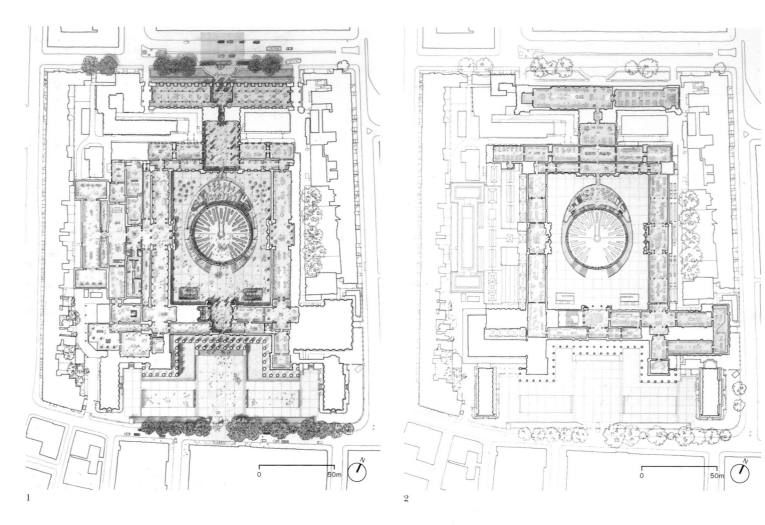

1
2

The Great Court of the British Museum is one of London's lost spaces. The court was originally intended to be the heart of the museum but was almost immediately filled in with the insertion of the new Reading Room of the British Library and associated book stacks. This caused congestion in the Front Hall and constricted circulation throughout the museum. The departure of the library provides a magnificent opportunity to recapture this central inner courtyard.

The Great Court will be enclosed with a lightweight glazed roof and will be entered from the principal level of the museum, through Smirke's great Ionic portico. The museum's Centre for Education and new ethnographic galleries will be located beneath this main level.

Bookshops, a restaurant and cafés will be on level 2 and the mezzanine levels above.

Continued

1 Master plan, main level 2
2 Master plan, level 6
3 Aerial view of current museum
4 CAD view of Great Court roof
5 Aerial view with roof over Great Court

3

4

5

These mezzanines, elliptical in plan, are centred on the restored drum of the Reading Room, which is encircled by a pair of great staircases. The original Smirke facades of the courtyard will also be restored and the southern portico reinstated. The Great Court will be open to the public from early in the morning to late at night, creating a major new public space for London. The forecourt in front of the museum will be freed from cars and re-landscaped to form a new external space.

6

7

9

8

6   CAD view of Great Court
7   Model view of Great Court roof
8   CAD view of Great Court
9   Section model of Great Court

Bio-medical Sciences Building, Imperial College

Design/Completion 1994/1998
London, England
Imperial College London
15,680 square metres
Concrete trough slab structure
Concrete, high-performance glass, aluminium, stone, brick, carpet, vinyl

Fosters were recently commissioned to design the new Basic Medical Sciences and Biological Sciences Building at Imperial College, providing new accommodation, facilities and technology for specific user groups.

The single most important factor in building a new educational and research facility is its flexibility: it must be able to change without affecting the building's design integrity. The facility must be able to accommodate continuing developments in technology, new research projects and new scientific outlooks, and must be an asset in the recruitment of senior researchers.

The aim with the Bio-medical Sciences Building was to produce a cost-effective and environmentally efficient building which could accommodate a complex range of services and systems. The structure and servicing had to be flexible, to respond to the changing requirements of research groups during the life of the building. It was also an opportunity to create a landmark building to reflect the international excellence of Imperial College and to revitalise the very heart of the college.

1

2

1 Plan view of model
2 CAD view of interior
3 Photomontage of exterior

3

Daewoo Research and Development Headquarters

Design/Completion 1995/2000
Seoul, South Korea
Daewoo Electronics
155,000 square metres
Steel and concrete composite structure
Steel, concrete, glass, aluminium, stone

The skeletal form of the tapered 166-metre-high tower will be a combined steel and concrete structure. The main steel frame is made up of two inner columns and two outer columns that follow the curved facade of the building. Steel outrigger trusses provide stability at intervals up the structure. Where these occur, triple-height sky gardens are created with external terraces. A slender steel and concrete central core runs the full height of the building distributing all services to the long, column-free office floors.

The tower will have an energy-efficient triple-layered facade with adjustable blinds to prevent solar gain and openable windows for partial natural ventilation. High-speed lifts up one side of the building stop at the triple-height garden levels. High-speed passenger lifts on the northern facade will animate the building at night and provide magnificent views over Seoul.

Continued

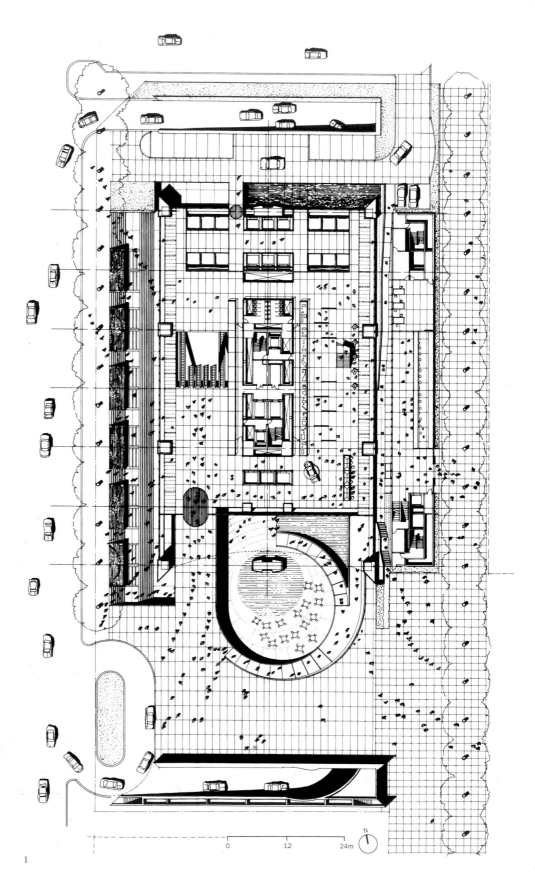

1

0   12   24m

2

1 Ground floor plan
2 Model view

There are extensive basements over the whole site. The upper levels form an internal public plaza containing shops, cafés, restaurants, a fitness centre and an auditorium, while the lower levels contain car parking, plant and loading bays. A calm public plaza leads down to double-height lower ground level garden areas.

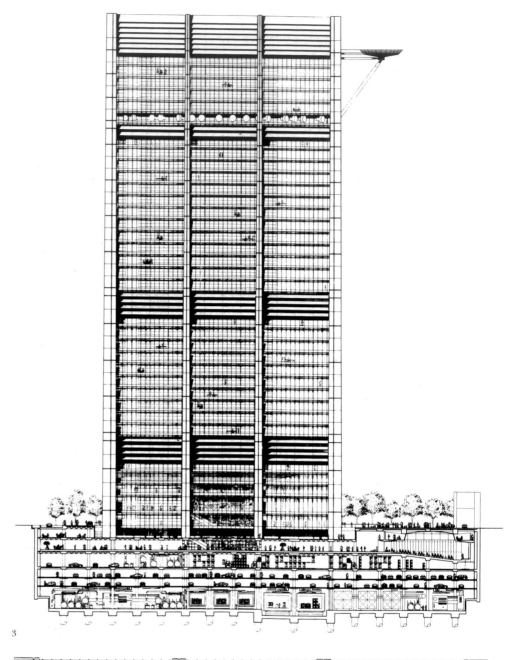

3

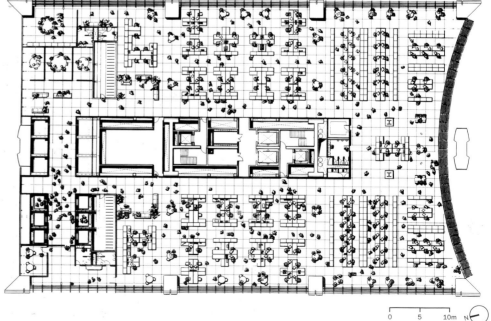

4

0   5   10m   N

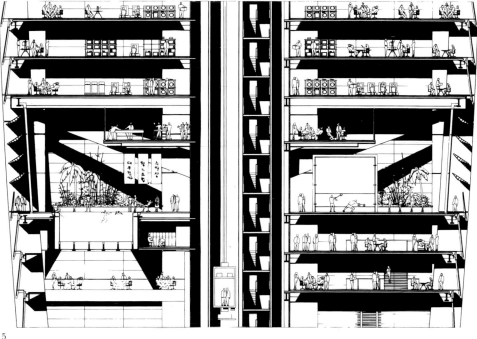

5

3   West elevation
4   Level 21 furniture layout
5   Cross-section through fitness centre
6   Design team building the model
7&8   Model view

6

7

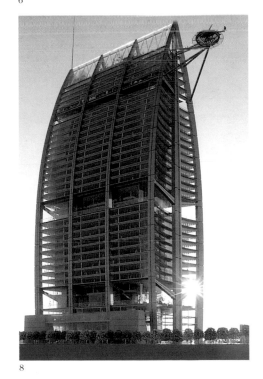

8

Scottish Exhibition and Conference Centre

Design/Completion 1995/1997
Glasgow, Scotland
Scottish Exhibition Centre Ltd
13,000 square metres
Steel roof structure, concrete and steel composite floor slabs, reinforced concrete walls
Steel, concrete, aluminium, glass, blockwork, carpet, plasterboard

In recent years, the conference business has become increasingly important, but there are few high-quality facilities in Britain which accommodate more than 2,000 delegates. The existing Scottish Exhibition and Conference Centre (SECC) in Glasgow was originally constructed as an exhibition centre, with five halls of varying sizes. With the addition of a new 3,000-seat conference centre, the SECC becomes one of only four centres in Europe with this capacity.

The building's form is derived from the internal planning, which wraps accommodation around the auditorium in layers. The roof encloses the resultant form in a sequence of elegant shells, reminiscent of a cluster of ships' hulls, reflecting the centre's position

Continued

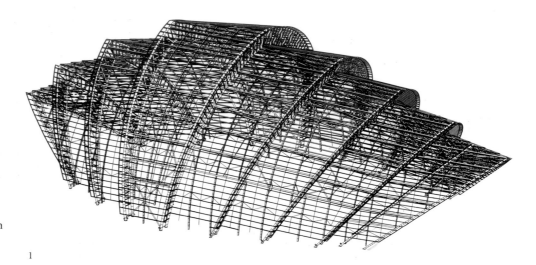

1

2

200

1 CAD perspective of roof structure
2&3 Construction views
4 Long section

3

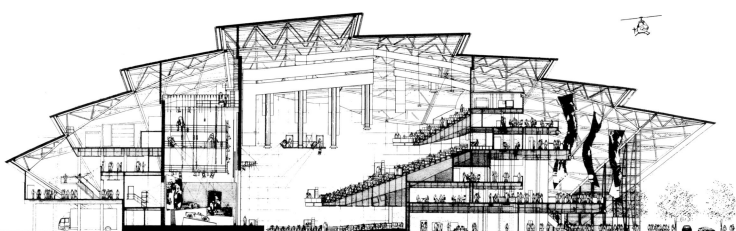

4

beside the river Clyde on what was once the Queen's Dock. Slots between the shells allow daylight to flood into the foyer spaces around the auditorium. These slots articulate the form of the building to create memorable impressions by day and by night.

The new conference centre will become a landmark and strengthen Glasgow's reputation as a major European city. Most importantly, it will enable the city to compete with conference and exhibition facilities around the world.

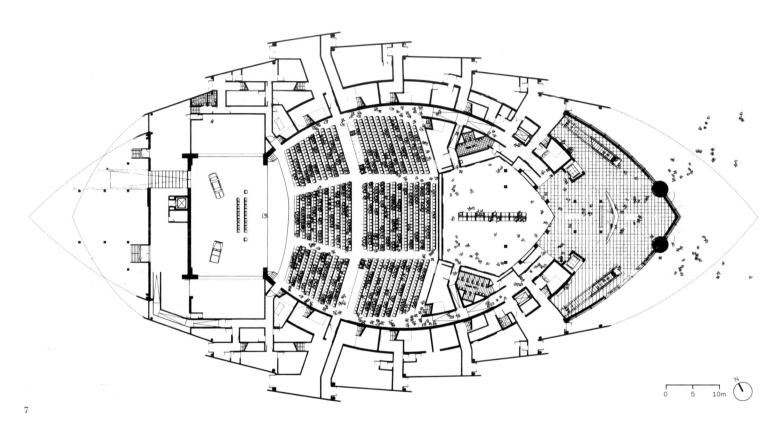

7

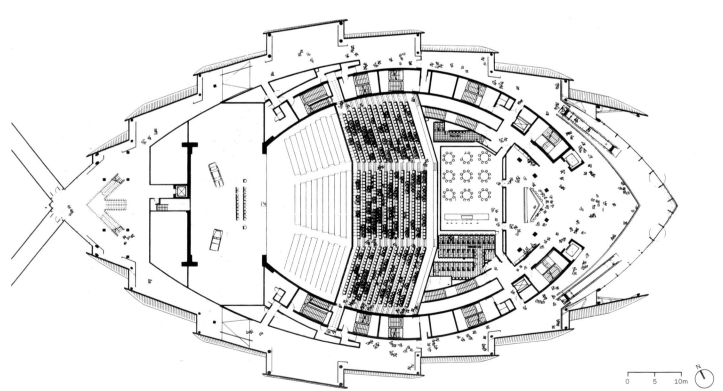

8

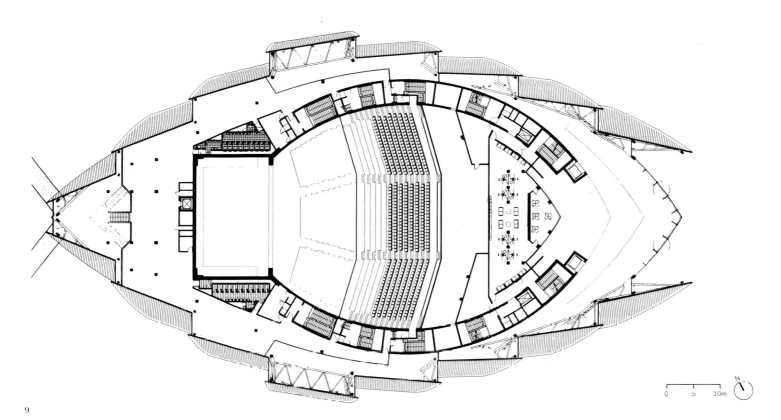

9

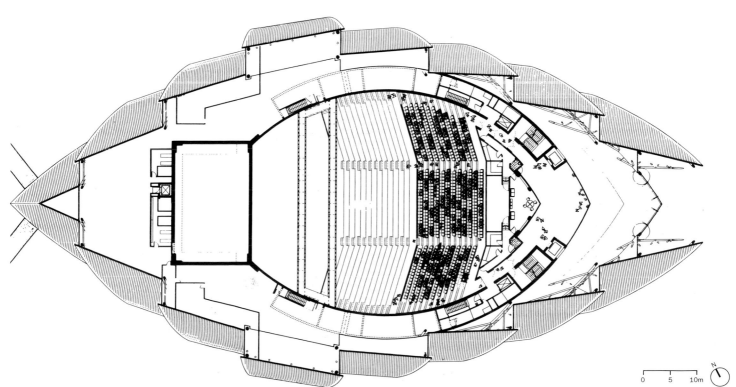

10

London Millennium Tower

Competition 1996
City of London
Trafalgar House Property Ltd (a subsidiary of Kvaerner)
240,000 square metres
Composite concrete and steel columns
Concrete, steel, glass, aluminium, stone

The site is free from many of the constraints which normally limit the scale of development in the City of London. It lies within an existing cluster of high-rise buildings which include the Lloyd's Building, the Commercial Union Tower and the NatWest Tower. As a result, the 95-storey London Millennium Tower, at 385 metres, will be taller than both the highest office building in Britain, Canary Wharf (244 metres), and Europe's tallest tower, the Foster-designed Commerzbank headquarters in Frankfurt (300 metres).

With a curved, free-form plan, the building will constantly change in appearance as different qualities of sunlight hit the continuous curves of the glass facade. The top of the building divides into two tail fins of different heights. The glazed, double-height ground floor lobby has an open plaza in front of it, creating a feeling of spaciousness and light at ground level.

1

1&2   Model view

3

4

3   Photomontage: night view from Canary Wharf
4   Photomontage: view from St Paul's Cathedral
5   Model view
6   Norman Foster concept sketch

5

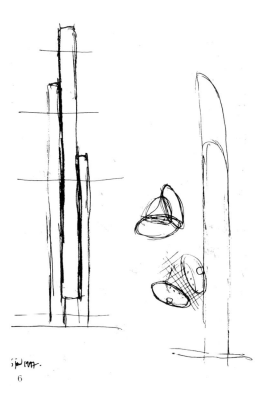

6

Millennium Bridge

Competition 1996
London, England
Financial Times
300 metres long
Steel and concrete
Stainless steel, concrete and timber decking

Foster and Partners, together with the sculptor Sir Anthony Caro and engineers Ove Arup & Partners, have designed a new Millennium Bridge across the Thames. It will be London's first new river crossing for more than 100 years and the capital's first pedestrian bridge. It will link St Paul's Cathedral to the north and the area around the new Tate Gallery of Modern Art and the Globe Theatre to the south. It will also open up new views of London, and in particular of St Paul's Cathedral, undisturbed by vehicles and city noise.

The bridge itself describes an elegant arc which touches down lightly in the passage of Peter's Hill and terminates grandly on Bankside. The main vertical connections are by gentle ramps; small flights of steps interlock with the ramps to create a curved ziggurat which integrates bridge, sculpture, ramps and viewing platform.

Continued

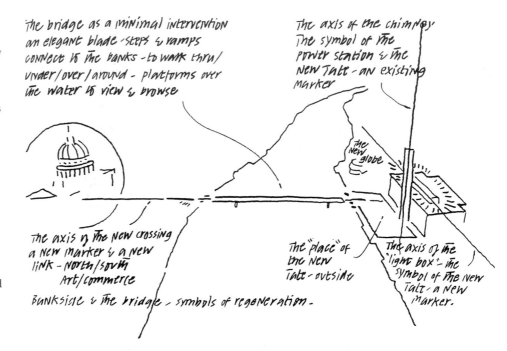

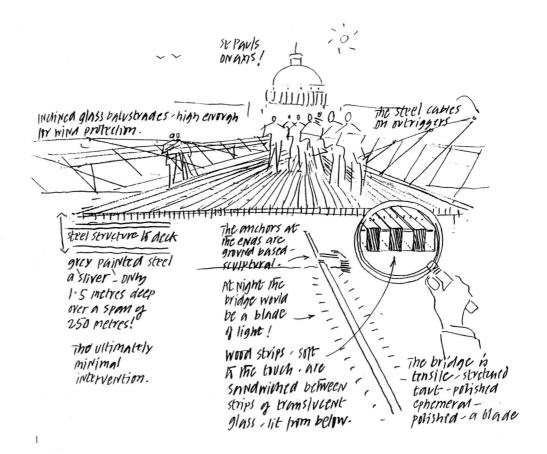

1   Norman Foster concept sketches
2&3 Model views
4   Plan view of model

3

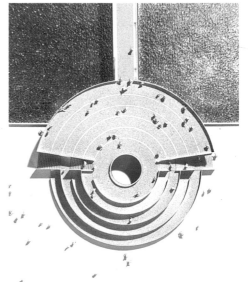

2

4

5

6

The "feel" of the bridge is tactile and sensory. The edge trim, lighting grilles, handrails and balustrades are of stainless steel, while the deck is made of timber (an ecologically sensitive hardwood that will bleach with age). The sound of movement on the wooden decks is part of the experience of the crossing, as is the smell of the wood when wet or drying.

5   View with City of London behind
6   CAD view towards St Pauls Cathedral
7   Detail model view

7

Design Centre Essen

Design/Completion 1992/1997
Zollverein, Essen, Germany
Bauhutte Zeche Zollverein Schacht XII GmbH
5,000 square metres
Existing boilerhouse for coal mine: steel structure with brick infill
Steel, glass, concrete, stainless steel

Conservation, like architecture, is subject to swings in taste and fashion. In Britain, the conservation movement grew up to protect ancient buildings from over-zealous acts of restoration. The challenge is to adapt old buildings without fundamentally altering their original character. This is the problem presented at Zollverein near Essen, where a magnificent but redundant coal-mining complex has been adapted to new uses. In particular, the old powerhouse—a masterpiece of industrial archaeology— has been remodelled as a centre for industrial design without destroying the fabric of the building or its interiors.

The powerhouse forms the centrepiece of an extraordinary group of buildings, all of which share a common vocabulary of brown and red-painted exposed steel I-beams, with an infill of industrial glazing and red brick. One of the large boilers of the powerhouse has been preserved intact as a specimen of the technology of its time; the remaining area has been converted into exhibition space for the new German Design Centre.

1

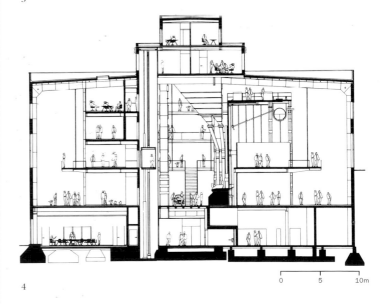

1 Central corridor
2 Central corridor
3 Exhibition space within old boiler
4 Cross-section

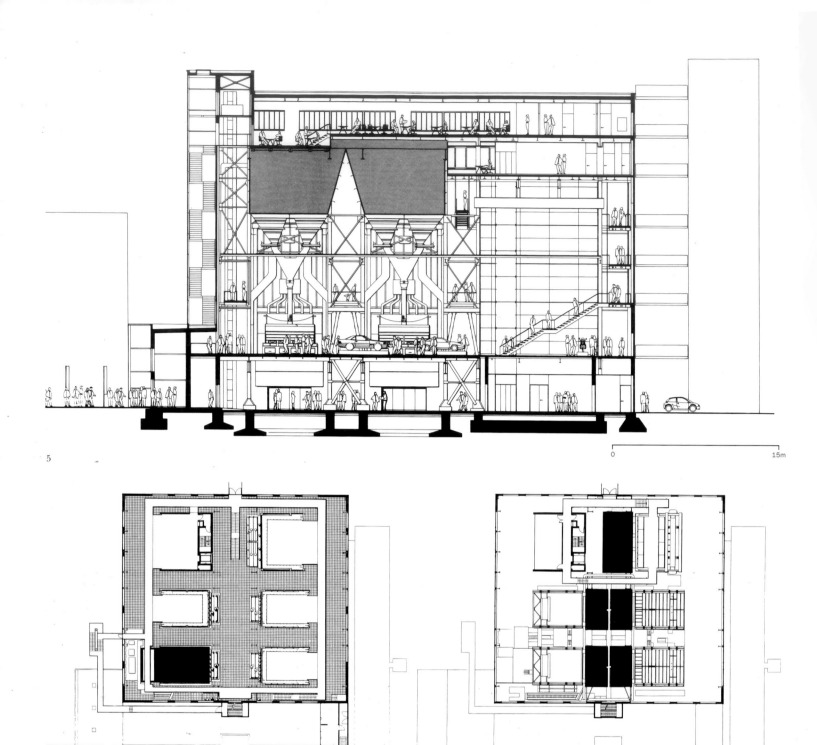

5

0   15m

6

7

0   5   10m

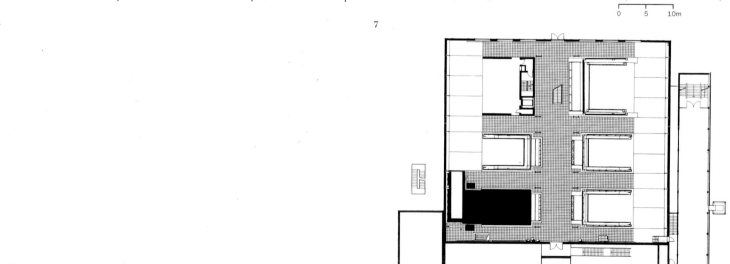

8

5   Long section
6   Level 2 plan
7   Level 4 plan
8   Level 1 plan

Faculty of Management, Robert Gordon University

Design/Completion 1994/1998
Aberdeen, Scotland
The Robert Gordon University
12,000 square metres
Concrete structure with metal decking
Grey granite, concrete, glass, anodised aluminium, steel, carpet

The Robert Gordon University, currently spread across eight teaching sites in the city of Aberdeen in north-east Scotland, was keen to consolidate into a single campus on one of its sites straddling the banks of the River Dee.

The master plan which has been developed creates a linear pedestrian street connecting the faculty buildings. The design of the buildings has been sensitive to the valuable landscape resources on the site, seeking to strengthen existing tree lines and enhance the microclimate for the benefit of the site and the people using it.

The first faculty building to be relocated on the site is the new Faculty of Management, located on an undulating south-facing slope on the north bank of the river. The building form responds to the dramatic landscape with its curved roof profile. Its design is a low-cost solution to the requirements of the academic users and will take advantage of natural light and ventilation.

1

2

3

4

1   Perspective illustration
2   Model of campus master plan
3   CAD view at night
4   Concept sketch

Prado Museum Extension

Competition 1996
Madrid, Spain
Materials: Granite, glass

The Prado houses one of the world's best art collections in a fine building whose capacity allows only 11 per cent of the works to be displayed at any time. The competition brief suggested resolving the museum's space problems through the creation of underground links between the main Villanueva building and other buildings around the site; Foster and Partners took a different approach.

The scheme opens up the entire perimeter of the historic building as public space, with a sculpture garden, terraces, cafés and a substantial entrance area on the north side.

A new wing, respecting the historic facades, wraps around the north and east perimeter, exploiting the depth of the road along the east side, so that much of the rooftop becomes a ground level plaza. The extension, which improves circulation and adds ample capacity, is generous in height and natural light, and contains permanent and temporary exhibition spaces, plus all administration, ticketing, restaurant, library, storage and restoration facilities. The whole of the historic building is thus released for displays.

1

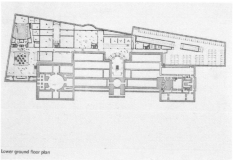

Lower ground floor plan

2

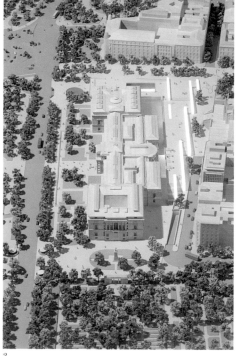

3

4

5

6

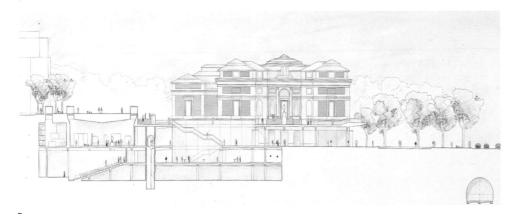

7

8

1 Aerial view of site model
2 Level minus 1 floor plan
3 Aerial view of model from the south
4 View from the north-east
5 View of proposed temporary exhibition gallery
6 View of Paseo del Prado
7 Cross-section through entrance and courtyard
8 Aerial view from the west

National Botanic Garden of Wales, Middleton Hall

Design/Completion 1996/1999
Middleton Hall, Cardiff, Wales
National Botanic Garden of Wales
Great Glass House: steel and glass structure
Steel, glass, concrete, stone

The gardens will be located in the 560-acre park of the former 18th century Middleton Hall, now demolished. Many of the park's original features will be restored, including its five historic lakes. At the heart of the gardens will be the new Great Glass House. In addition, a series of new buildings to house the ticket office, restaurants and the children's education centre audio visual displays have been carefully designed to integrate with the landscape proposals.

A careful balance has to be struck between modern design and restoration, between aesthetic and scientific planting, and between pure pleasure and pure research.

The Great Glass House is a 95-metre by 55-metre elliptical dome set into the landscape and enclosing one major volume. It will incorporate five specific temperature and humidity zones corresponding to different regions of Africa. The domed roof is a simple continuous form with a minimal structure; it therefore admits the maximum amount of light whilst minimizing maintenance.

Continued

1

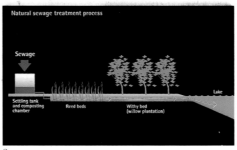

Natural sewage treatment process

Sewage

Settling tank and composting chamber

Reed beds

Withy bed (willow plantation)

Lake

2

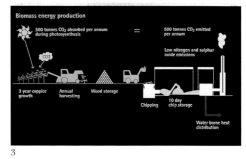

Biomass energy production

500 tonnes CO_2 absorbed per annum during photosynthesis = 500 tonnes CO_2 emitted per annum

Low nitrogen and sulphur oxide emissions

3 year coppice growth

Annual harvesting

Wood storage

Chipping

10 day chip storage

Water borne heat distribution

3

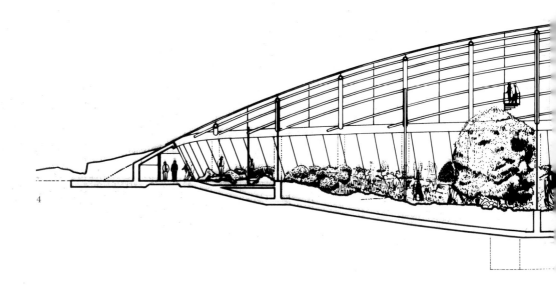

4

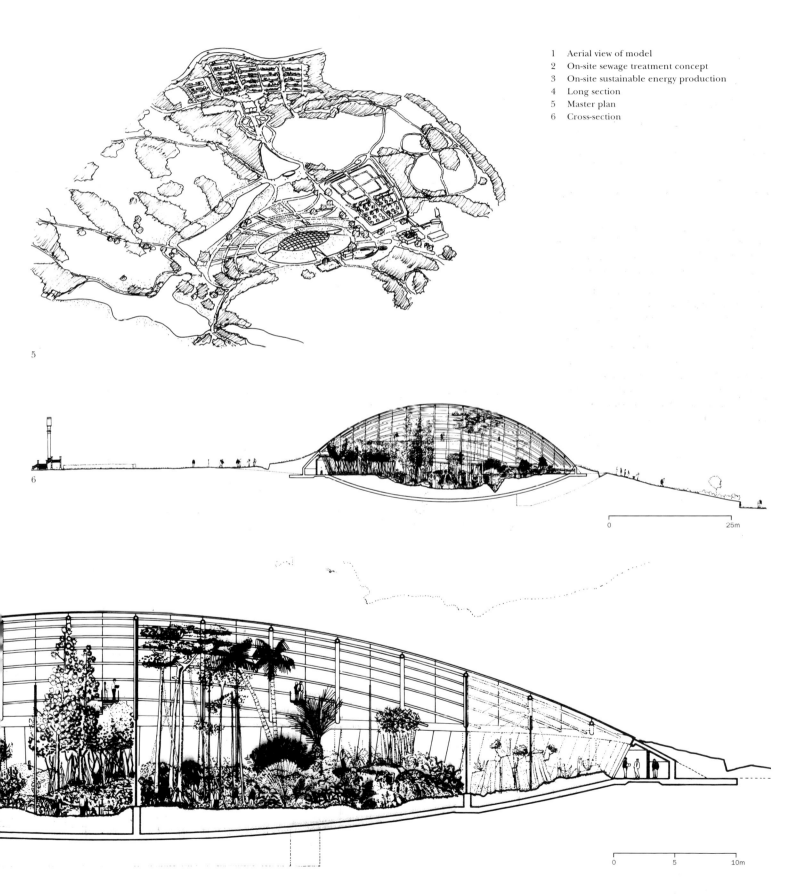

1 Aerial view of model
2 On-site sewage treatment concept
3 On-site sustainable energy production
4 Long section
5 Master plan
6 Cross-section

5

6

The glass house is solid on the north face, responding to the cold in winter; retractable sun shading will be incorporated to prevent overheating in summer.

New buildings will form a composition that is considerate to the park's historic setting and will use local materials where appropriate.

7

8

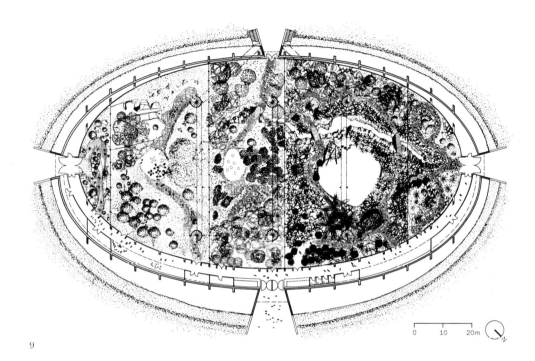

9

10

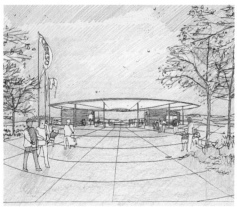

11

7 View of interior
8 Model showing interior of Great Glass House
9 Plan
10 CAD view of glass house interior
11 Artist's impression of entrance building

Center for Clinical Sciences Research, Stanford University

Design/Completion 1995/1999
Palo Alto, California, USA
Stanford University, California
20,000 square metres
Concrete, steel
Concrete, aluminium, steel, stone

The Center for Clinical Sciences Research will provide new laboratory and office space for the medical research programs of the Stanford School of Medicine, and for its faculty students and investigators. The school has recognised the need for a building that responds to emerging trends in biomedical research, whilst allowing expansion in several research endeavours.

A modular system has been devised for the building, with two wings mirrored around a central courtyard flooded with natural light. This allows all departments to be within close proximity of one another, gathered around a common central space. Each office will overlook the courtyard through curved bay windows with an overhead screen of louvres to provide shading from strong daylight. Horizontal circulation between the wings will be via lightweight bridges spanning the courtyard on each level. Glass lifts will connect all levels vertically.

The scheme responds sympathetically to the surrounding buildings, with a horizontal line of louvres at the third floor level to match the cornice line established by the neighbouring Hospital and School of Medicine Complex.

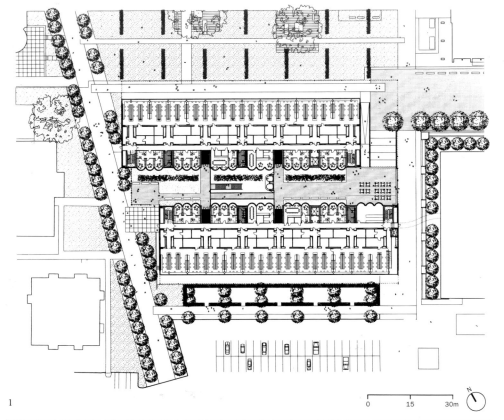

1

0   15   30m

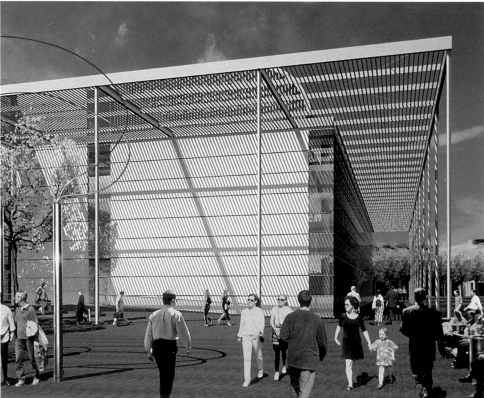

1   Site Plan
2   CAD view, exterior
3   CAD view, interior
4   CAD view, interior

2

222

3

4

Wembley Stadium

Design 1996
London, England
English National Stadium Trust
80,000-seat capacity
Concrete and steel

The new national stadium, which would replace the existing 1920s stadium in Wembley, north London, is designed to provide the ultimate spectator experience. Features would include improved comfort, access and sightlines as well as a retractable roof.

The scheme makes a special feature of Wembley's famous twin towers: they would form an impressive gateway through which spectators would pass into the stadium environment. The towers will be moved to allow the stadium to be spun through 90 degrees, creating a new north–south axis. This orientation minimizes sun glare. The shape of the stadium resembles the "Wembley Wave", giving the seating a sweeping curve which also improves sightlines.

Using the latest laser technology, the external skin would become a giant projection screen to provide a wall of moving images for the spectators outside the stadium. Retractable seating over the perimeter running track allows spectators to get closer to the on-pitch action. Two-thirds of seats would have armrests and could be fitted with in-seat information systems.

1

2

224

1 Photomontage of stadium on match day
2 CAD view showing video screen skin
3 Artist's impression of aerial view

3

World Squares for All

Design/Completion 1996/2000
Trafalgar Square and Parliament Square, London, England
Westminster City Council, Department of National Heritage,
Government Office for London, London Transport, The Royal
Parks Agency, English Heritage, The Parliamentary Works
Directorate, Traffic Director of London
Urban landscaping scheme

This competition-winning project to transform the quality of the environment in the historic heart of Westminster seeks to enhance and improve public access to the area including Trafalgar Square, Parliament Square, Whitehall, Horse Guards Parade, Westminster Abbey and the Palace of Westminster.

Additionally, the initiative includes preserving and enhancing the setting of 170 listed buildings and a world heritage site in the political, religious and ceremonial heart of the nation. The aim is to improve facilities for Londoners and tourists, reduce bus journey times, create better access to the London Underground and improve safety for cyclists and pedestrians.

More than 100 local or interested groups will be consulted during the 13-month study period and, on the basis of that consultation, a recommendation will be made as to the most appropriate and popular scheme.

The design team has focused on 10 key ideas for the area which aim to improve the key spaces and connections to the river. It is anticipated that substantial elements of the approved plan would be implemented by the year 2000, subject to the necessary funding being obtained.

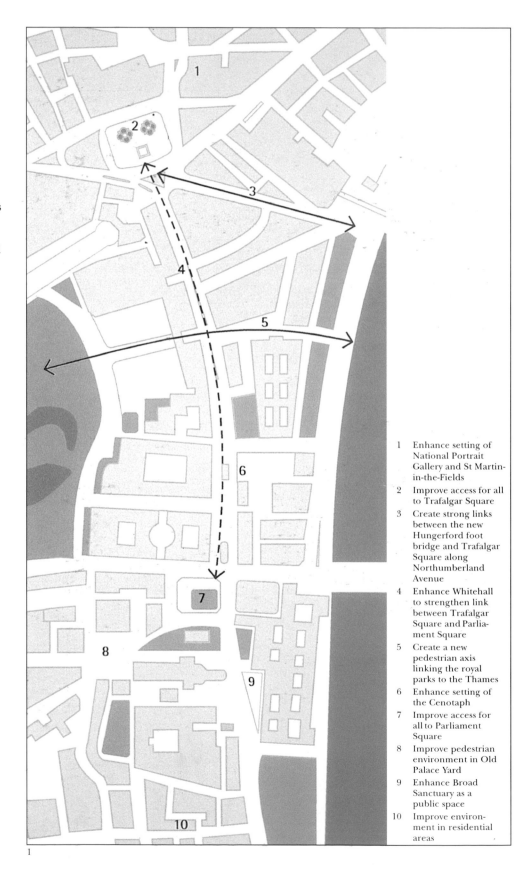

1 Enhance setting of National Portrait Gallery and St Martin-in-the-Fields

2 Improve access for all to Trafalgar Square

3 Create strong links between the new Hungerford foot bridge and Trafalgar Square along Northumberland Avenue

4 Enhance Whitehall to strengthen link between Trafalgar Square and Parliament Square

5 Create a new pedestrian axis linking the royal parks to the Thames

6 Enhance setting of the Cenotaph

7 Improve access for all to Parliament Square

8 Improve pedestrian environment in Old Palace Yard

9 Enhance Broad Sanctuary as a public space

10 Improve environment in residential areas

1

2

3

1 Site plan
2 Trafalgar Square as it is today
3 The Cenotaph as it is today

Product Design

Throughout the history of the Foster office, the design of specific building elements has played a fundamental role in the overall success of the firm's finished projects. As the practice has grown, the design and development of individual products, furniture and interiors not related to specific architectural projects has also expanded. This service benefits from the multidisciplinary nature of the practice.

Throughout the conceptual design process, a dialogue is developed with the client and with external manufacturing experts to discuss and explore options for achieving the best concept for the new product, interior or range of components.

Proprietary products are often neither suitable nor flexible enough for a defined need, so new products have been developed by the practice. For example, cable management "totems" (boxes containing electrical and communications sockets) were developed when no suitable product could be found off the shelf.

Continued

1

2

3

4

5

6

7

1   Banking teller desks detail
2   Hongkong Bank: banking hall teller desks
3   Mock-up of check-in desks
4   Mock-up of check-in desks being checked by client
5   Check-in desks, Stansted Airport
6   Kite chair for Tecno
7   Norman Foster sketch: kite chair for Tecno

They were installed at the Foster office and are now manufactured in Germany by Akermann.

A range of purpose-designed door handles and door furniture has also recently been launched by the Italian manufacturer Fusital. The inspiration for the shape of the handle came from a bird-shaped handle that Norman Foster happened across on the door of Magdeburg Cathedral in Germany. Architects typically prefer the "D" handle style which, although being aesthetically pleasing with its clean, simple and functional lines, is nevertheless alien to the shape of the hand in a way the Magdeburg handle was not.

Work continues on tableware, storage systems, book stacks (already installed in buildings such as Cranfield Library, Carré d'Art, Nîmes and Cambridge Law Faculty), chairs, tables, desk systems, exhibition stands and electronic goods.

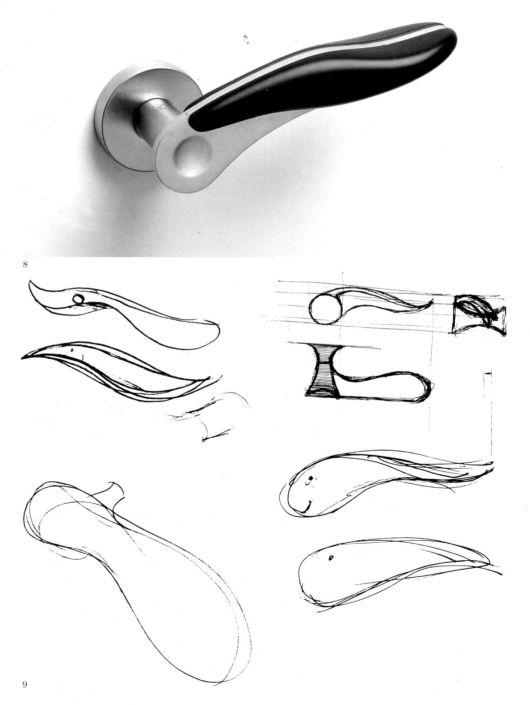

8

9

10

11

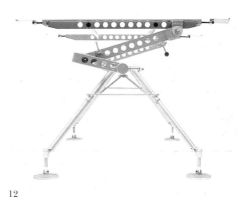

12

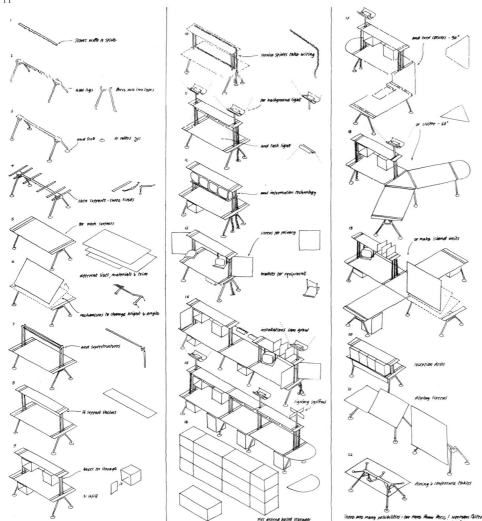

13

PROFILE

Biographies

NORMAN FOSTER
DipArch (Manc) MArch (Yale) RIBA

Born in 1935, Norman Foster studied architecture and city planning
at Manchester University. After graduating in 1961 he was awarded
a Henry Fellowship to Yale University, where he subsequently received
a Masters degree. He worked on urban renewal and master planning
projects on the east and west coasts of the USA before starting his own
private practice in 1963. Norman Foster has received honorary degrees
and fellowships from many universities and institutions around the world.
He was knighted in the Queen's Honours List in 1990 and received the
Royal Gold Medal in 1983 and AIA Gold Medal in 1994. He is a member
of numerous academies and has taught and lectured extensively. He is a
past vice-president of the Architectural Association and a visiting examiner
for the RIBA.

Spencer de Grey DipArch MA (Cantab) CBE

Born in 1944, Spencer de Grey studied architecture at Cambridge
University under Sir Leslie Martin, graduating in 1966. His international
student competition entry for a new city in Finland was highly placed.
He then worked for the London Borough of Merton and was responsible
for the design and construction of the Borough's first Middle School.
He joined Foster Associates in 1973, and in 1979 established the
company's Hong Kong office. In 1981 he returned to London to become
Director in charge of the Third London Airport, and he became a Partner
in 1991. In 1995 he was made a Trustee for the Royal Botanical Gardens
in Kew.

David Nelson MA (RCA)

Born in 1951, David Nelson studied three-dimensional design at
Loughborough College of Art and at Hornsey College of Art, specializing
in furniture/industrial design, and gained a Diploma in Art and Design
with distinctions. He then studied at the Royal College of Art,
Environment Design School, gaining a Masters degree. He subsequently
received a travelling scholarship to study town planning in Northern Italy.
He joined Foster Associates in 1976, and in 1979 started with the
Hongkong and Shanghai Bank project team, initially with responsibility
for internal systems and later as co-ordinator of design. He was made
a Director in 1984, returned from Hong Kong in 1986 and was made
a Partner in 1991.

Graham Phillips BArch (Hons) (Liverpool) RIBA HKIA

Born in 1947, Graham Phillips studied architecture at Liverpool University
and graduated with first class honours in 1971. He worked for a year in
Toronto and later joined Arup Associates in a multidisciplinary team
working on a variety of large projects. He joined Foster Associates in 1975
and developed special skills in the fields of project management, cost
control and contract administration. He became a Resident Director in
Hong Kong in 1980, and is a member of HKIA and an Authorised Person.
On his return from Hong Kong in 1986 he became Managing Director of
the practice and was made a Partner in 1991.

Ken Shuttleworth DipArch (Dist) RIBA HonDDes

Born in 1952, Ken Shuttleworth studied at Leicester Polytechnic and received a Diploma in Architecture with distinction in 1977. He became a registered architect in 1978, having joined Foster Associates in 1974 while still a student. After an architectural study tour of the USA and Canada he returned to Foster Associates in 1977. He was appointed a Director of Foster and Partners in 1984 and worked in Hong Kong on the Hongkong and Shanghai Bank Headquarters where he was responsible for all aspects of the design. In 1986 he returned from Hong Kong and was made a Partner in 1991. In 1994 he received an honorary doctorate from De Montfort University.

Barry Cooke FCA

Born in 1950, Barry Cooke qualified as a chartered accountant in 1973. He joined Ernst and Whinney in West Africa and worked as financial consultant to the Minister of Finance of Liberia. He transferred to the Paris office in 1976 before returning to London to join Balfour Beatty as chief accountant for the Power Transmission Division dealing with overseas construction projects. He joined the Trafalgar House Group in 1978 where he became financial controller of Cementation International. In 1984 he transferred to Gammon Construction in Hong Kong where he was responsible for all accounting, data processing and project finance. He joined Foster Associates in 1988, becoming a partner in 1997, and is involved in every aspect of the practice.

Stefan Behling Dipl. -Ing. Architect

Born in Germany in 1962, Stefan gained his diploma from Aachen University and was still studying when he joined Foster Associates in 1987 to work on the King's Cross Master Plan. He was project architect for several projects in Duisburg, in the Ruhr district of Germany, where he developed an interest in the environmental and ecological aspects of buildings. He worked on the Reichstag competition in Berlin and helped to develop the energy concept for the building. With his wife, Sophia, he has written a book about solar energy, *Sol Power*. He became a Director in 1996 and is currently a part-time professor at the University of Stuttgart.

Brandon Haw BSc (Hons) MArch (Princeton) RIBA

Born in 1960, Brandon Haw studied at London University, gaining a Bachelors degree with honours and a Masters degree from Princeton University. He worked for five years in New York, both freelance and with various practices. Brandon joined Foster Associates in 1987 to work on the competition-winning master plan for King's Cross, becoming an Associate in 1988 and a Project Director in 1991. As Resident Director in the Frankfurt office for two years, he shared the responsibility of managing a team of 40 working on the Commerzbank Headquarters. He returned to the UK in 1994 to direct a major mixed-use development in Riyadh, Saudi Arabia for the King Faisal Foundation. He was made a Director in 1995.

Robin Courtland Partington BA (Hons) BArch (Hons) (Liverpool) RIBA

Born in 1960, Robin Courtland Partington studied architecture at Liverpool University and graduated with honours. He joined Foster Associates in 1984 and worked on the competition-winning scheme for the Carré d'Art in Nîmes. He was made an Associate in 1988 and a Project Director in 1989. He was made a Director of the practice in 1992 and helped set up the Hong Kong office. He was Director in charge of the Düsseldorf office and shared responsibility for the Commerzbank Headquarters in Frankfurt. He is now responsible for the Glasgow office as well as overseas projects such as the new headquarters for the Emirates Bank in Dubai.

Paul Kalkhoven Ir

Born in Holland in 1955, Paul Kalkhoven studied architecture and town planning at the Technical University of Delft. He graduated as Bouwkundig Ingenieur, and has since registered as an architect in the Netherlands and the UK. He worked for five years in London before joining Foster Associates in 1985 to work on transportation and infrastructure projects. He was made an Associate in 1987 and a Project Director in 1991. At one time he was responsible for four design teams working on the Commerzbank Headquarters project in the Frankfurt office. More recently he has been co-ordinating a wide range of projects in western Germany. He was made a Director of the practice in 1995.

Andrew Miller DipArch (Glos)

Born in 1944, Andrew Miller studied architecture at Gloucestershire College of Art and Design where he graduated in 1981. He joined YRM International Hong Kong and worked on several large projects there including the Mass Transit Railway Island Line project. He joined Foster Associates Hong Kong in 1983, working on the Hongkong and Shanghai Bank Headquarters. As a Project Director in the Tokyo office in 1987, he worked on projects such as Century Tower and Millennium Tower in Japan. He became Resident Director of Foster Japan in 1992 and a Director of Foster and Partners, London in 1996 after returning from Japan.

John Silver BSc (Hons) DipArch (London) RIBA

Born in 1961, John Silver studied at the Bartlett School of Architecture, London University and graduated with first class honours. After qualifying as a chartered architect he joined YRM in 1982 and his Sinclair Research Centre competition entry was exhibited at the Royal Academy in 1984. Shortly afterwards he joined Foster Associates to work on Stansted Airport, which he followed through to completion in 1991, and on a second satellite building in 1993. He became a Project Director in 1989, working on the Cambridge University Law Faculty and the Fréjus Lycée, and in 1994 he was made a Director of the practice. Recently he has been Director responsible for several large office projects.

Mark Sutcliffe DipArch (Poly) RIBA

Born in 1944, Mark Sutcliffe graduated in architecture from the London Polytechnic, joining Team 4 in 1963. He subsequently worked in the USA and in London with the GLC and Borough of Camden. He joined Foster Associates in 1969 and was made an Associate in 1971 to lead the Willis Faber & Dumas project. For two periods between 1976 and 1992 he worked as a freelance architect specializing in project management, rejoining Foster Associates in 1983 as a Project Director for the BBC Headquarters and in 1992 as Resident Director in Frankfurt. He is now a Director of the practice with specific responsibility for project management.

Chronological List of Buildings & Projects

*Indicates work featured in this book
(see Selected Works).
†Indicates winner of national or
international competition.

1997 Department Store for Selfridges, Glasgow

1996 World Squares for All Master Plan for Central London†*

1996 Millennium Bridge, London†*

1996 Office Development for Citibank, London

1996 Stadium Design and Master Plan for Wembley Stadium, London†*

1996 Arsta Bridge, Sweden†

1996 Oxford University Library, Oxford

1996 Redevelopment of Treasury Offices, London

1996–1997 Offices for Slough Estates, Ascot and Slough

1996 International Rail Terminal, St Pancras, London

1996 London Millennium Tower Mixed-use Development, City of London*†

1996 National Botanic Gardens of Wales, Middleton Hall, Wales*

1995 London Underground Interchange, Greenwich

1995 Center for Clinical Sciences Research, Stanford University, California, USA†*

1995 Office and Showroom for Samsung Motors, South Korea†

1995 Multimedia Centre, Hamburg, Germany†

1995 Door Furniture for Fusital, Italy*

1995–1997 Swimming Pool and Fitness Centre, Stanmore, Middlesex

1995 World Port, Rotterdam, Netherlands

1995 I.G. Metall Headquarters, Frankfurt, Germany

1995 Bank Headquarters, Dubai

1995 Private House in Connecticut, USA

1995 Cladding System for Technal, France

1995 Daewoo Research and Development Headquarters, Seoul, South Korea*

1995–1997 Scottish Exhibition and Conference Centre, Glasgow*

1995 Solar City Linz, Austria

1995 Master Plan, Solar City Regensburg, Germany

1995 Criterion Place Development, Leeds†

1995 Club House, Silverstone Race Track, Silverstone

1995 Jiu Shi Tower, Shanghai, China

1995 Murr Tower Offices, Beirut†

1995 Offices for LIFFE, Spitalfields, London

1994 Telecommunications Facility, Santiago de Compostela, Spain*

1994 Master Plan and Faculty of Management for Robert Gordon University, Aberdeen*

1994 Visions for Europe, Düsseldorf, Germany

1994–1998 Bio-medical Sciences Building, Imperial College, London*

1994 Great Court, British Museum, London*†

1994 Cardiff Bay Opera House, Cardiff, Wales

1994 New Offices at Holborn Circus, London

1994 Grande Stade, St Denis, Paris, France

1994 Centre de la Mémoire, Oradour sur Glanes, France

1994 Casino-Kursaal Oostende, Belgium

1994 Bangkok Airport, Thailand

1994 Zhongshan Guangzhou, Retail and Office Development, China†

1994–1996 SeaLife Centre, Birmingham

1994–1995 SeaLife Centre, Blankenberge, Belgium

1993 Al Faisaliah Complex, Riyadh, Saudi Arabia*†

1993 Millau Bridge, Millau, France*†

1993 Office and Railway Development, Kuala Lumpur, Malaysia

1993–1995 Forth Valley Community Village, Scotland*

1993 Headquarters for ARAG 2000, Düsseldorf, Germany

1993 Master Plan for Lisbon Expo, Portugal†

1993 Master Plan for Corfu, Greece

1993 Hong Kong Convention and Exhibition Centre, Hong Kong

1993 London School of Economics Library, London

1993 Tennis Centre, Manchester

1993 Headquarters for Timex, Connecticut, USA

1993 Street Lighting for Decaux, France

1993–1997
MTR Platform Edge Screens, Signage and Furniture, Hong Kong

1993–1995
Wind Turbine Energy Generator, Germany

1993–1998
HACTL Cargo Building for New Airport Chek Lap Kok, Hong Kong

1993–1998
Congress Centre, Valencia, Spain*

1993 South Kensington Millennium Project—Albertopolis†

1993 National Gallery of Scottish Art, Glasgow

1993 Oresund Bridge, Copenhagen, Denmark

1993 Imperial War Museum, Hartlepool†

1993 Exhibition Halls , Villepinte, Paris, France

1993 Urban Design at Porte Maillot, Paris, France

1993 Medieval Centre for Chartres, France

1993 Masterplanning Studies for Gare d'Austerlitz Station, Paris, France

1993 New Headquarters for Credit du Nord, Paris, France

1992–1996
Offices for Electricité de France, Bordeaux, France*

1992–1998
Kowloon Canton Railway Terminal, Hong Kong*

1992–1994
Solar Electric Vehicle, Kew Gardens, London*

1992 Competition for New York Police Academy, New York, USA

1992 Headquarters Factory and Warehouse for Tecno, Valencia, Spain

1992–1999
New German Parliament, Reichstag, Berlin, Germany*†

1992 Offices, Tower Place, City of London

1992 Yokohama Master Plan, Japan

1992 Competition for Business Park, Berlin, Germany†

1992 Manchester Olympic Bid Master Plan†

1992–1993
Refurbishment and addition to the Hamlyn House, Chelsea

1992 Spandau Bridge, Berlin, Germany

1992–1996
Thames Valley Business Park, Reading†

1992 Station Poterie, Rennes, France

1992–1994
Addition to Joslyn Art Museum, Omaha, Nebraska, USA*†

1992–1994
School of Physiotherapy, Southampton

1992–1994
Private House in Germany*

1992 High-bay Warehouse, Lüdenscheid, Germany

1992 Master Plan for Lüdenscheid, Germany

1992 Houston Museum of Fine Arts, USA

1992–1997
Ground Transport Centre, Chek Lap Kok, Hong Kong*

1992–1998
Airport at Chek Lap Kok, Hong Kong*†

1992–1993
Marine Simulator, Rotterdam, Netherlands

1992 Master Plan for Rotterdam, Netherlands

1992 Master Plan for Imperial College, London

1992 Competition for World Trade Centre, Berlin, Germany

1992–1992
Clore Theatre, Imperial College, London

1992 Shops and Franchises for Cacharel, France

1992 Musée de la Préhistoire, Gorges du Verdon, France*†

1992–1997
Design Centre, Essen, Germany*

1991   Three Private Houses in Japan

1991–1992
Cladding System for Jansen
Vegla Glass

1991   Master Plan for Greenwich,
London

1991   Inner Harbour Master Plan,
Duisburg, Germany*†

1991   Paint Factory, Frankfurt
Colloquium, Frankfurt, Germany

1991–1997
Commerzbank
Headquarters, Frankfurt,
Germany*†

1991   Gateway Office Building to
Spitalfields Redevelopment,
London

1991–1993
Lycée Albert Camus, Fréjus,
France*†

1991   Napp Laboratories, Cambridge

1991   University of Cambridge Institute
of Criminology, Cambridge

1991   Office Building for Stanhope
Properties, London

1991   New Headquarters and Retail
Building for Sanei Corp.,
Makuhari, Japan

1991–1996
New Headquarters for
Agiplan, Mulheim, Germany

1991–1993
New Headquarters for
Obunsha Corp., Yarai Cho, Tokyo,
Japan

1991–1998
Canary Wharf Station,
Jubilee Line Extension, London*†

1991–   Viaduct for Rennes, France†

1991–1993
Motor Yacht for Japanese
Client*

1990–1993
House for M. Bousquet,
Corsica, France

1990   Master Plan for Berlin, Germany

1990   Master Plan for Cannes, France

1990   Master Plan for Nîmes, France

1990–1995
University of Cambridge,
Faculty of Law, Cambridge*†

1990   Office Building for Fonta,
Toulouse, France

1990   Refurbishment of Brittanic House,
City of London

1990   Hotel du Département, Marseilles,
France

1990   Congress Hall, San Sebastian, Spain

1990   Trade Fair Centre, Berlin, Germany

1989   Millennium Tower, Tokyo, Japan*

1989   Offices for Stanhope Properties,
Chiswick Park, London

1989–1992
Cranfield University Library,
Bedfordshire*†

1989   Planning Studies for the City
of Cambridge

1989   Office Building DS2 at Canary
Wharf, Docklands, London†

1989   Apartments and Offices,
New York, USA

1989–1991
Street Furniture for Decaux,
Paris, France*

1989   Terminal 5 Heathrow Airport,
London

1989–1991
British Rail Station, Stansted
Airport, Stansted, Essex

1989   Technology Centres, Edinburgh
and Glasgow, Scotland

1989   Office Building for Jacob's
Island Co., Docklands, London

1988–1990
ITN Headquarters,
London*

1988–1996
Micro-Electronic Centre,
Duisburg, Germany*

1988–1993
Business Promotion Centre
and Telematic Centre, Duisburg,
Germany*

1988   Sackler Galleries, Jerusalem, Israel

1988–1991
Crescent Wing, Sainsbury
Centre for Visual Arts, University
of East Anglia, Norwich*

1988–1992
Telecommunications Tower,
Torre de Collserola, Barcelona,
Spain*†

1988–1995
Bilbao Metro, Spain*†

1988   City of London Heliport

1988   Shop for Esprit, Sloane Street,
London

1988 Contract Carpet and Tile Design
for Vorwerk, Switzerland

1988 Kansai Airport, Japan

1988 Pont D'Austerlitz, Bridge across the
River Seine, Paris, France

1988 Offices for Stanhope Securities,
London Wall, City of London

1988 Holiday Inn, The Hague,
Netherlands

1987 Hotel and Club, Knightsbridge,
London

1987 Redevelopment Master Plan, King's
Cross, London*†

1987–1989
Riverside Housing and Light
Industrial Complex, Hammersmith,
London

1987–1991
Century Tower, Bunkyo ku,
Tokyo, Japan*

1987–1992
Private Houses in Japan*

1987–1989
Offices for Stanhope Securities,
Stockley Park, Uxbridge, Middlesex

1987–1997
American Air Museum,
Imperial War Museum, Duxford*

1987 Turin Airport, Italy

1987 Hotel for La Fondiaria,
Florence, Italy

1987 Shopping Centre near
Southampton for Savacentre

1987 Bunka Radio Station, Yarai Cho,
Tokyo, Japan

1987 Paternoster Square
Redevelopment, London

1986–1990
Riverside Development,
Apartments and Offices for Foster
and Partners

1986 Salle de Spectacles, Nancy, France

1986 Headquarters for Televisa,
Mexico City, Mexico

1986 Shop for Katharine Hamnett,
Brompton Road, London*

1986 New York Marina, New York, USA

1985–1991
Sackler Galleries, Royal Academy
of Arts, London*

1985–1987
Furniture System for Tecno,
Milan, Italy

1985 New Offices for IBM at Greenford,
Middlesex

1984–1993
Carré d'Art, Nîmes, France*†

1984–1986
IBM Head Office Major Refit,
Cosham, Hampshire

1982 BBC Radio Headquarters,
London*†

1982 Autonomous Dwelling
(with Dr Buckminster Fuller), USA

1982 Headquarters of Humana Inc.,
Louisville, Kentucky, USA

1981 Foster Associates Office, Great
Portland Street, London

1981 Internal Systems, Furniture
for Foster Associates

1981–1986
National Indoor Athletics Stadium,
Frankfurt, Germany†

1981–1991
London's Third Airport,
Stansted, Essex*

1981 Billingsgate Fish Market, London

1980–1983
Renault Distribution Centre,
Swindon, Wiltshire*

1980 Planning Studies for Statue Square,
Hong Kong

1980 Students Union Building,
University College, London

1979–1985
Hongkong and Shanghai Banking
Corporation Headquarters,
Hong Kong*†

1979 Granada Entertainment Centre,
Milton Keynes

1979 Shop for "Joseph", Knightsbridge,
London

1978 London Gliding Club,
Dunstable Downs

1978–1979
Foster Residence,
Hampstead, London

1978 Proposals for International Energy
Expo, Knoxville, USA

1978 Open House Community Project,
Cwmbran, Wales

1978 Whitney Museum Development
Project, New York, USA

1977–1979
Technical Park for IBM,
Greenford, Middlesex

1977–1979
Transportation Interchange
for LTE, Hammersmith, London

1976–1977
Master Plan for St Helier Harbour,
Jersey

1975–1976
Regional Planning Studies for
Island of Gomera, Canary Islands

1975   Fred Olsen Gate Redevelopment,
Oslo, Norway

1974–1978
Sainsbury Centre for Visual Arts,
University of East Anglia, Norwich,
Norfolk*

1974–1975
Palmerston Special School,
Liverpool

1974   Country Club and Marina, Son,
Norway

1974   Travel Agency for Fred Olsen
Limited, London

1974   Offices for Fred Olsen Limited,
Vestby, Norway

1973–1975
Low-rise Housing, Bean Hill,
Milton Keynes Development
Corporation

1973–1974
Headquarters for VW Audi NSU
& Mercedes Benz, Milton Keynes

1973–1977
Aluminium Extrusion Plant for
SAPA, Tibshelf, Derby

1972–1973
Orange Hand Boys Wear Shops
for Burton Group

1972–1973
Modern Art Glass Limited,
Thamesmead, Kent

1971–1973
Special Care Unit, Hackney,
London

1971   Foster Associates Studio, London

1971   Theatre for St Peter's College,
Oxford

1971   Climatroffice
(project with Buckminster Fuller)

1971–1972
Retail and Leisure Studies,
Liverpool, Exeter and
Badhoevedorp, Netherlands

1970–1975
Willis Faber & Dumas Head Office,
Ipswich, Suffolk*

1970–1971
Fred Olsen Limited Passenger
Terminal, Millwall

1970–1971
Computer Technology Limited,
Hemel Hempstead, Hertfordshire

1970–1971
IBM Pilot Head Office,
Cosham, Hampshire*

1970   Air-Supported Structure for
Computer Technology Limited,
Hertfordshire

1969   Factory Systems Studies

1969   Master Plan for Fred Olsen
Limited, Millwall Docks

1968–1969
Fred Olsen Limited Amenity
Centre, Millwall

1967   Newport School Competition

1965–1966
Reliance Controls Limited,
Swindon, Wiltshire

1965   Housing for Wates, Coulsden

1965   Henrion Studio, London

1964   Forest Road Extension, East
Horsley, Surrey

1964   Mews Houses, Murray Mews,
Camden Town, London

1964   Waterfront Housing, Cornwall

1964–1966
Skybreak House, Radlett,
Hertfordshire

1964–1966
Creek Vean House, Feock,
Cornwall*

1964   Cockpit, Cornwall

Awards & Competitions

Large Architectural Practice of the Year Award
The *Building* Award
1997

American Academy of Arts and Sciences Award
Norman Foster
1996

International Competition Winner
Millennium Bridge
London, England
1996

Bund Deutscher Architekten Bezirksgruppe Rechter Niederrhein
Auszeichnung guter Bauten
Micro-Electronic Centre
Duisburg, Germany
1996

Competition Winner
World Squares for All
London, England
1996

International Competition Winner
Redeveloping the Baltic Exchange
The London Millennium Tower
London, England
1996

International Competition Winner
Bridge over the Arstaviken
Sweden
1996

International Competition Winner
Viaduct at Millau
Millau, France
1996

Medal and Honorary Diploma
International Academy of Architecture
Solar City Regensburg
1996

I.D. Design Distinction Award in Concepts
I.D. Annual Design Review
Solar Electric Vehicle, Hybrid Electric Vehicle
1996

Construction Personality of the Year
The *Building* Award
Sir Norman Foster
1996

Large Architectural Practice of the Year Award
The *Building* Award
1996

Man of the Year Award
MIPIM
Sir Norman Foster
1996

Competition Winner
Wembley Stadium and Master Plan
London, England
1996

International Competition Winner
Center for Cancer and Neuroscience Research
Stanford University
California, USA
1996

International Competition Winner
Multimedia Centre
Hamburg, Germany
1996

International Competition Winner
Offices and Showroom for Samsung Motors
South Korea
1995

Competition Winner
Criterion Place Office Development
Leeds, England
1995

Premio Radio Correo Award
Bilbao Metro
Bilbao, Spain
1995

AIA Regional Architecture Award
Joslyn Art Museum Addition
Omaha, Nebraska, USA
1995

AIA State Architecture Award
Joslyn Art Museum Addition
Omaha, Nebraska, USA
1995

Disabled Access Award
Steiger Schwanentor
Duisburg Harbour
Duisburg, Germany
1995

Minerva Design Awards
Solar Electric Vehicle
1995

British Safety Council Safety Award
Foster and Partners
1995

Architectural Practice of the Year
The *Building* Award
1995

Queen's Award for Export Achievement
Foster and Partners
1995

Civic Trust Award
Cranfield University Library
Bedfordshire, England
1995

***Designweek* Award for Product Design**
Solar Electric Vehicle
1995

CICA CAD Drawing Award
Holborn Place Offices
London, England
1994

Hilight Award
Best European Interior Lighting Scheme
Architectural Review
Marine Simulator Centre
Rotterdam, Netherlands
1994

Officer of the Order of Arts and Letters
Ministry of Culture, France
Sir Norman Foster
1994

International Competition Winner
Murr Tower
Beirut
1994

International Competition Winner
British Museum Redevelopment
London, England
1994

International Competition Winner
Al Faisaliah Complex
Riyadh, Saudi Arabia
1994

British Steel Colorcoat Award Runner Up
Cranfield University Library
Bedfordshire, England
1994

Interiors USA Award
Marine Simulator Centre
Rotterdam, Netherlands
1994

BBC Design Awards
London's Third Airport
Stansted, Essex, England
1994

The Society of Heating, Air Conditioning and Sanitary Engineers of Japan Award
Century Tower
Tokyo, Japan
1994

Conference Award
Intelligent Award Promotion
Century Tower
Tokyo, Japan
1994

Bund Deutsche Architekten Bezirksgruppe Ruhr Award
Business Promotion Centre
Duisburg, Germany
1994

Gold Medal
American Institute of Architects
Sir Norman Foster
1994

Building of the Year
Eastern Electricity Commercial Property Award
Cranfield University Library
Bedfordshire, England
1993

Best Public Development Award
Eastern Electricity Commercial Property Award
Cranfield University Library
Bedfordshire, England
1993

Best Architectural Project
Eastern Electricity Commercial Property Award
Cranfield University Library
Bedfordshire, England
1993

Special Commendation, Building Services System
Eastern Electricity Commercial Property Award
Cranfield University Library
Bedfordshire, England
1993

Financial Times **Architecture Award**
London's Third Airport
Stansted, Essex, England
1993

Financial Times **Architecture Award**
Cranfield University Library
Bedfordshire, England
1993

Concrete Society Award
Cranfield University Library
Bedfordshire, England
1993

International Competition Winner
Master Plan for Lisbon Expo
1993

Interiors **(USA) Award**
Carré d'Art
Nîmes, France
1993

Interiors **(USA) Award**
Cranfield University Library
Bedfordshire, England
1993

RIBA Regional Award
Cranfield University Library
Bedfordshire, England
1993

Special Award
Bedfordshire Design Award
Cranfield University Library
Bedfordshire, England
1993

Building Award
British Construction Industry Award
Cranfield University Library
Bedfordshire, England
1993

Supreme Award
British Construction Industry Award
Cranfield University Library
Bedfordshire, England
1993

British Council for Offices Award
Offices at Stockley Park
1993

The Architecture FAD Award
Torre de Collserola
Barcelona, Spain
1993

The Opinion FAD Award
Torre de Collserola
Barcelona, Spain
1993

Benedictus Award, USA
For the innovative use of laminated glass
London's Third Airport
Stansted, Essex, England
1993

Minerva Design Award
Sackler Galleries
London, England
1993

Special Mention
Marble Architectural Award
Sackler Galleries
London, England
1993

Citation Award
International Association of Lighting Designers
Crescent Wing, Sainsbury Centre for Visual Arts
University of East Anglia
Norwich, England
1993

International Competition Winner
Manchester Olympic Bid Master Plan
1993

Lighting Design Award
Cranfield University Library
Bedfordshire, England
1993

International Competition Winner
New German Parliament, Reichstag
Berlin, Germany
1993

The Architecture and Urbanism Award
City of Barcelona
Telecommunications Tower
Torre de Collserola, Barcelona, Spain
1993

Best Building of the Year Award
RIBA
Sackler Galleries
London, England
1993

National Architecture Award
RIBA
London's Third Airport
Stansted, Essex, England
1992

National Architecture Award
RIBA
Sackler Galleries
London, England
1992

Civic Trust Award
Stansted Airport Terminal
Stansted, Essex, England
1992

Civic Trust Award
Crescent Wing, Sainsbury Centre for
Visual Arts
University of East Anglia
Norwich, England
1992

AJ/Hilight Lighting Award
Commendation
London's Third Airport
Stansted, Essex, England
1992

Structural Steel Award
London's Third Airport
Stansted, Essex, England
1992

Structural Steel Award
Sackler Galleries
London, England
1992

Energy Efficiency Award
Royal Institute of Chartered Surveyors
Award
London's Third Airport
Stansted, Essex, England
1992

British Construction Industry Award
Sackler Galleries
London, England
1992

Interiors (USA) Award
Sackler Galleries
London, England
1992

International Competition Winner
Business Park
Berlin, Germany
1992

Regional Architecture Award
RIBA
Sackler Galleries
London, England
1992

Regional Architecture Award
RIBA
ITN Headquarters
London, England
1992

Regional Architecture Award
RIBA
Crescent Wing, Sainsbury Centre for
Visual Arts
University of East Anglia
Norwich, England
1992

Regional Architecture Award
RIBA
London's Third Airport
Stansted, Essex, England
1992

Concrete Society Award
London's Third Airport
Stansted, Essex, England
1992

National Dryline Wall Award
Sackler Galleries
London, England
1992

**Premio Alcantara Award for Public Works
in Latin American Countries**
Torre de Collserola
Barcelona, Spain
1992

BCS Award
Century Tower
Tokyo, Japan
1992

Merit Award
Institution of Civil Engineers
Sackler Galleries
London, England
1992

**Commendation
Brunel Award Madrid**
British Rail Station, Stansted Airport
Stansted, Essex, England
1992

International Competition Winner
Addition to the Joslyn Art Museum
Omaha, Nebraska, USA
1992

Building of the Year Award
The Royal Fine Art Commission and
Sunday Times
Sackler Galleries
London, England
1992

Arnold W. Brunner Memorial Prize
American Academy and Institute of Arts
and Letters, New York
Sir Norman Foster
1992

Best Building Award
British Council for Offices
ITN Headquarters
London, England
1992

Car Park Special Award, Rural Category
English Tourist Board
Stansted Airport Car Park
1992

Mansell Refurbishment Award
Sackler Galleries
London, England
1992

**Lightweight Metal Cladding Association
Award**
Century Tower
Tokyo, Japan
1992

Award for New Technology
Nikkei Business Publications
Century Tower
Tokyo, Japan
1992

International Competition Winner
Airport at Chek Lap Kok
Hong Kong
1992

International Competition Winner
Musée de la Préhistoire
Gorges du Verdon, France
1992

Landscaping Award
British Association of Landscape
Industries
London's Third Airport
Stansted, Essex, England
1991

Energy Management Award
British Gas
London's Third Airport
Stansted, Essex, England
1991

National Childcare Facilities Award
London's Third Airport
Stansted, Essex, England
1991

Special Award
Institution of Structural Engineers
Century Tower
Tokyo, Japan
1991

**Business and Industry Panel for the
Environment Award**
London's Third Airport
Stansted, Essex, England
1991

**Silver Jubilee Planning Award for
Achievement**
Royal Town Planning Institute
London's Third Airport
Stansted, Essex, England
1991

Supreme Award
British Construction Industry
London's Third Airport
Stansted, Essex, England
1991

First Prize
Colorcoat Building Award
Car park and canopies at Stansted Airport
1991

International Competition Winner
Commerzbank Headquarters
Frankfurt, Germany
1991

International Competition Winner
Duisburg Inner Harbour Master Plan
Duisburg, Germany
1991

International Competition Winner
Lycée Albert Camus
Fréjus, France
1991

**Aluminium Imagination Architectural
Award**
Offices at Stockley Park
1991

**Aluminium Imagination Architectural
Award**
ITN Headquarters
London, England
1991

**Aluminium Imagination Architectural
Award**
London's Third Airport
Stansted, Essex, England
1991

Gold Medal
French Academie de Paris
Norman Foster
1991

**Mies van der Rohe Pavilion Award for
European Architecture 1990**
London's Third Airport
Stansted, Essex, England
1991

Knighthood
Norman Foster
Queen's Birthday Honours List
1990

Competition Winner
University of Cambridge, Law Faculty
Library
1990

RIBA Trustees Medal
Willis Faber & Dumas Head Office
Ipswich, Suffolk, England
1990

International Competition Winner
Viaduct
Rennes, France
1990

The Chicago Architecture Award
Norman Foster
1990

British Construction Industry Award
Offices at Stockley Park, Uxbridge
1989

Competition Winner
Cranfield University Library
Bedfordshire, England
1989

Interiors **(USA) Award**
Shop for Esprit
London, England
1988

PA Innovations Award
Hongkong and Shanghai Banking
Corporation Headquarters
Hong Kong
1988

**Quaternario Award for Innovative
Technology in Architecture**
Hongkong and Shanghai Banking
Corporation Headquarters
Hong Kong
1988

International Competition Winner
Bilbao Metro
Bilbao, Spain
1988

International Competition Winner
Telecommunications Tower, Torre de
Collserola
Barcelona, Spain
1988

International Competition Winner
King's Cross Master Plan
London, England
1987

Japan Design Foundation Award
Norman Foster
1987

Design Centre Award Stuttgart
Nomos Furniture for Tecno
Milan, Italy
1987

Premio Compasso d'Oro Award
Nomos Furniture for Tecno
Milan, Italy
1987

Special Award
Institution of Structural Engineers
Hongkong and Shanghai Banking
Corporation Headquarters
Hong Kong
1986

Structural Steel Award
Hongkong and Shanghai Banking
Corporation Headquarters
Hong Kong
1986

Marble Architectural Awards East Asia
Hongkong and Shanghai Banking
Corporation Headquarters
Hong Kong
1986

R.S. Reynolds Memorial Award
AIA
Hongkong and Shanghai Banking
Corporation Headquarters
Hong Kong
1986

First Prize
European Award for Industrial
Architecture, Hanover
Renault Distribution Centre
Swindon, Wiltshire, England
1986

International Competition Winner
Contemporary Arts Centre
Carré d'Art
Nîmes, France
1984

Honourable Mention
UIA Auguste Perret Prize for Applied
Technology in Architecture
1984

Architecture at Work Award
The *Financial Times*
Renault Distribution Centre
Swindon, Wiltshire, England
1984

Civic Trust Award
Renault Distribution Centre
Swindon, Wiltshire, England
1984

Structural Steel Award
Renault Distribution Centre
Swindon, Wiltshire, England
1984

The Royal Gold Medal for Architecture
1983

A*J*/Premier Architectural Award
Hongkong and Shanghai Banking
Corporation Headquarters
Hong Kong
1983

International Competition Winner
BBC Radio Headquarters
London, England
1982

International Competition Winner
National Indoor Athletics Stadium
Frankfurt, Germany
1981

Industrial Architecture Award
Commendation
The *Financial Times*
Offices for IBM
Greenford, Middlesex, England
1981

Commendation
Royal Institute of British Architects
Offices for IBM
Greenford, Middlesex, England
1981

Structural Steel Award Citation
Offices for IBM
Greenford, Middlesex, England
1980

Museum of the Year Award
Sainsbury Centre for Visual Arts
University of East Anglia
Norwich, Norfolk, England
1980

Ambrose Congreve Award
Sainsbury Centre for Visual Arts
University of East Anglia
Norwich, Norfolk, England
1980

6th International Prize for Architecture, Brussels
Sainsbury Centre for Visual Arts
University of East Anglia
Norwich, Norfolk, England
1980

International Competition Winner
Hongkong and Shanghai Banking
Corporation Headquarters
Hong Kong
1979

British Tourist Board Award
Sainsbury Centre for Visual Arts
University of East Anglia
Norwich, Norfolk, England
1979

R.S. Reynolds Memorial Award
Sainsbury Centre for Visual Arts
University of East Anglia
Norwich, Norfolk, England
1979

Structural Steel Finniston Award
Sainsbury Centre for Visual Arts
University of East Anglia
Norwich, Norfolk, England
1978

Royal Institute of British Architects Award
Sainsbury Centre for Visual Arts
University of East Anglia
Norwich, Norfolk, England
1978

Royal Institute of British Architects Award
Willis Faber & Dumas Head Office
Ipswich, Suffolk, England
1977

Royal Institute of British Architects Award
Palmerston Special School
Liverpool, England
1977

R.S. Reynolds Memorial Award
Willis Faber & Dumas Head Office
Ipswich, Suffolk, England
1976

International Prize for Architecture
Palmerston Special School
Liverpool, England
1976

Business and Industry Panel for the Environment Award
Willis Faber & Dumas Head Office
Ipswich, Suffolk, England
1976

Industrial Architecture Award
The *Financial Times*
Modern Art Glass Limited
Thamesmead, Kent, England
1974

Structural Steel Award
IBM Advance Head Office
Cosham, Hampshire, England
1972

Royal Institute of British Architects Award
IBM Advance Head Office
Cosham, Hampshire, England
1972

Industrial Architecture Award
The *Financial Times*
Computer Technology Limited
Hemel Hempstead, Hertfordshire,
England
1971

Industrial Architecture Award
The *Financial Times*
Fred Olsen Limited Amenity Centre
Millwall, England
1970

Architectural Design Project Award
Fred Olsen Limited Amenity Centre
Millwall, England
1969

Royal Institute of British Architects Award
Creek Vean House
Feock, Cornwall, England
1969

Industrial Architecture Award
The *Financial Times*
Reliance Controls Limited
Swindon, Wiltshire, England
1967

Project Award
Architectural Design
Reliance Controls Limited
Swindon, Wiltshire, England
1966

Project Award
Architectural Design
Housing for Wates
Coulsden, England
1965

Project Award
Architectural Design
Waterfront Housing
Cornwall, England
1964

Bibliography

Selected Books and Exhibition Catalogues

Abel, Chris et al. *Norman Foster*. Japan: A+U Monograph, 1987.

Banham, Reyner. *Design by Choice*. London: Academy Editions, 1982.

Benedetti, Aldo. *Norman Foster*. Bologna: Nichola Zanichelli, 1987; Zürich: Verlag für Architektur Artemis, 1990; Madrid: Gustavo Gilli, 1994.

Best, Alastair. *Foster Associates: Six Architectural Projects 1975–1985*. Norwich: Sainsbury Centre for Visual Arts, 1985.

Best Alastair, et al. *Foster and Partners: Architects Designers and Planners*. London: Foster and Partners, 1996.

Blaser, Werner (ed.). *Norman Foster Sketches*. Basel: Birkhäuser Verlag, 1992.

Blaser, Werner (ed.). *Norman Foster Sketches*. Revised edn. Basel: Birkhäuser Verlag, 1993.

Bramante, Gabriele. *Willis, Faber & Dumas Building: Foster Associates*. London: Phaidon Press, 1993.

Brawne, Michael. *The Architecture of Information: Venice Biennale 1996*. London: The British Council, 1996.

Chaslin, Francois, Lavalou, Armelle & Hervet, Frederique. *Norman Foster: Une Volonte du Fer*. Paris: Electa Moniteur, 1986.

Col·legi d'Arquitectes de Catalunya (eds). *Norman Foster: Works and Projects 1981–1988*. Spain: Quaderns Monografia (Spain) Editorial/Gustavo Gilli, 1988.

Foster Associates (eds). *Reichstag Berlin*. Berlin: Aedes Galerie, 1994.

Foster Associates. RIBA Publications. London, 1978.

Foster Associates (eds). *Selected Works 1962–1984*. Manchester: Whitworth Art Gallery, 1984.

Foster Associates (eds). *Tre Temi Sei Progetti*. Florence: Electa, 1988.

Foster, Sir Norman & Partners (eds). *Deutsche Projekte: Sir Norman Foster and Partners*. Munich: Architekturgalerie München, 1995.

Fundacio San Benito de Alcantara (eds). *Norman Foster Arquitectura: Urbanismoy Medio Ambiente*. Spain: Fundacio San Benito de Alcantara, 1994.

Jencks, Charles. *Current Architecture*. London: Academy Editions, 1982.

Lambot, Ian (ed.). *Norman Foster: Team Four and Foster Associates Buildings and Projects 1964–1973, Volume 1*. Hong Kong: Watermark Publications, 1991.

Lambot, Ian (ed.). *Norman Foster: Foster Associates Buildings and Projects 1971–1978, Volume 2*. Hong Kong: Watermark Publications, 1990.

Lambot, Ian, (ed). *Norman Foster: Foster Associates Buildings and Projects 1978–1985, Volume 3*. Hong Kong: Watermark Publications, 1990.

Lambot, Ian (ed.). *Norman Foster: Foster Associates Buildings and Projects 1982–1989, Volume 4*. Hong Kong: Watermark Publications/Switzerland: Birkhäuser, 1996.

Lasdun, Denys (ed.). *Architecture in an Age of Scepticism*. Heinemann, 1984.

Moore, Rowan. *The Sackler Galleries*. Blueprint Extra 04. London: Wordsearch, 1992.

Powell, Kenneth. *Carré d'Art Nîmes*. Blueprint Extra 11. London: Wordsearch, 1994.

Powell, Kenneth. *Foster Associates Recent Works*. Architectural Monograph No. 20. London: Academy Editions/St Martin's Press, 1992.

Powell, Kenneth. *Norman Foster and the Architecture of Flight*. Blueprint Monograph. London: Wordsearch, 1992.

Powell, Kenneth. *Torre de Collserola, Barcelona*. Blueprint Extra 06. London: Wordsearch, 1992.

Sainz, Jorge et al. *Norman Foster*. Madrid: A & V Monografías de Arquitectura y Vivienda 38, 1992.

Suckle, Abby. *By Their Own Design*. New York: Whitney, 1980.

Sudjic, Deyan. *Foster, Rogers, Stirling*. London: Thames & Hudson, 1986.

Treiber, Daniel. *Norman Foster*. Switzerland: Birkhäuser, 1991; Paris: Eric Hazan, 1994; London: E&FN Spon, 1995.

Williams, Stephanie. *Hongkong Bank: The Building of Norman Foster's Masterpiece*. London: Jonathan Cape, 1989.

Yuroukov, Ilya & Kraichkova, Edith (eds). *Norman Foster Architect*. International Academy of Architecture Monograph No. 3. Varese, Italy: Arterigere, 1991.

Selected Journals and Periodicals

Abel, Chris et al. "Norman Foster." *Architecture and Urbanism* (special edition, May 1987).

Allain-Dupré, Elisabeth. "Gentle Giant: Foster's Carré d'Art in Nîmes." *Architecture Today* (June 1993).

Amery, Colin. "British Architecture Today." *Techniques et Architecture* (June/July 1992).

Banham, Reyner. "LL/LF/LE v Foster." *New Society* (9 November 1972).

Best, Alastair. "A Machine for Displaying Things." *Design* (July 1978).

Best, Alastair. "Legal Precedent." *Architectural Review* (March 1996).

Binney, Marcus. "Foster at the Academy." *Architectural Design* (March/April 1989).

Bjork, Sven. "Foster Associates." *AA Quarterly* (no. 1, 1973).

Brandolini, Sebastiano. "Ill Progetto del Grattacielo della Commerzbank a Francoforte." *Casabella* (no. 626, September 1995).

Cargill-Thompson, Jessica. "King Kong." *Building* (24 January 1997).

Castelli, Annamaria. "Foster Associates: Assembly without Composition." *Casabella* (no. 375, 1973).

Champenois, Michelle. "Foster à Nîmes." *L'Architecture d'Aujourd'hui* (June 1993).

Chevin, Denise. "Solar Architecture: Sun Worshipper." *Building* (7 January 1994).

Cook, Peter. "East Anglia Arts." *Architectural Review* (December 1978).

Davey, Peter et al. "Stansted Airport Special Issue." *Architectural Review* (May 1991).

Davey, Peter. "Renault Centre." *Architectural Review* (July 1983).

Davies, Colin. "Carré Culturel." *Architectural Review* (July 1993).

Davies, Colin. "High-tech Idealist." *Architecture* (May 1994).

Davies, Colin. "Logical Conclusion: Foster's Cranfield Library." *Architecture Today* (November 1992).

Dirk, Jan, Volker, Peereboom & Wintermans, Frank. "Appropriate Technology: Variaties op de Services Shed." *Wonen Tabk* (November 1982).

Doubilet, Susan & Fisher, Thomas. "Hongkong Bank Special Issue." *Progressive Architecture* (March 1986).

Emery, Marc. "Norman Foster." *L'Architecture d'Aujourd'hui* (February 1986).

Farelly, E.M. "Foster at the BBC." *Architectural Review* (May 1987).

Fisher, Thomas. "Industrial Design of Buildings." *Progressive Architecture* (December 1994).

"Foster and Partners." *Nikkei Architecture* (December 1996).

Foster Associates. "Industrial Materials and Techniques become Art." *Architectural Record* (mid-August 1979).

"Foster Associates." *Space Design* (special issue, no. 3, March 1982).

"Fostering the Arts." *Architects' Journal* (5 April 1978).

Foster, Norman. "Architects Approach to Architecture: Norman Foster." *RIBA Journal* (June 1970).

Foster, Norman. "Design for Living." *BP Shield* (March 1969).

Foster, Norman. "Exploring the Client's Range of Options." *RIBA Journal* (June 1970).

Foster, Norman. "Foster et Associés." *L'Architecture d'Aujourd'hui* (November/December 1973).

Foster, Norman. "New Buildings in Historic Contexts." *RIBA Journal* (February 1993).

Foster, Norman. "Philosophy of the WFD Building." *Architectural Design* (October 1977).

Foster, Norman. "Towards the Integration of New and Old." *Space Design* (no. 9, September 1993).

Foster, Norman. "Towards the Modern Vernacular." *Detail* (December/January 1993/4).

Galloway, David. "A Passion for Perfection." *Lufthansa Bordbuch* (May 1994).

Giovanni, Joseph. "Joslyn Art Museum Addition." *Architecture* (December 1994).

Glancey, Jonathan. "Fosterland." *The Independent* (18 December 1996).

Glancey, Jonathan. "Hongkong Bank." *Architectural Review* (May 1981).

Glancey, Jonathan. "Nimes Schemes." *Architectural Review* (May 1985).

Glancey, Jonathan. "The Eagle has Landed." *Architectural Review* (July 1983).

Glancey, Jonathan. "The Object Reassessed." *World Architecture* (April 1989).

Goldberger, Paul. "A Priest of High-Tech in a Classical Temple." *New York Times* (31 May 1992).

Goldstein, Barbara. "Designing the Means to the Social Ends." *RIBA Journal* (January 1978).

Hannay, Patrick. "Flight of Fancy." *Architects' Journal* (29 May 1991).

Haward, Birkin & Butt, Loren. "Fast Track Response." *Architects' Journal* (21 April 1982).

"Hongkong Bank." *Nikkei Architecture* (24 February 1986).

"Hongkong Bank." *Vision* (special issue, July 1985).

Ho, Tao & Matsuda, Naonori. "Hongkong Bank." *Process Architecture* (special issue, no. 70, 15 September 1986).

Hoyt, Charles K. "Brains and Brawn." *Architectural Record* (June 1992).

Irace, Fulvio. "Grattacielli a Hong Kong." *Abitare* (April 1986).

Jodidio, Philip (ed.). "Nîmes Carré d'Art." *Connaissance des Arts* (special issue, 1993).

Jodidio, Philip. "Technologie de Pointe pour une Architecture Optimiste." *Connaissance des Arts* (November 1983).

le Cuyer, Annette. "A Building that Succeeds in Losing Itself." *AIA Journal* (April 1981).

Manser, Jose. "British Technique." *Interiors* (May 1984).

Matthews, Robert. "Glass by Foster." *Building* (18 March 1983).

Maxwell, Robert. "The Urban Dimension in Recent Work by Norman Foster." *Casabella* (no. 557, May 1989).

McKean, John. "Gold Standard." *Architects' Journal* (30 March 1983).

Meade, Martin. "Norman Foster." *Beaux Arts* (February 1986).

Morgan, Peter. "Norman Foster." *Mandarin Oriental* (vol. 10, no. 1, March 1994).

Murray, Peter (ed.). "Foster Gold has Royal Approval." *RIBA Journal* (March 1983).

"My Kind of Space." *Architects' Journal* (28 October 1992).

Nakamura, Toshio (ed.). "Foster: Special Issue." *Architecture and Urbanism* (September 1975).

Nakamura, Toshio et al. "Hongkong Bank Special Issue." *Architecture and Urbanism* (June 1986).

Nakamura, Toshio (ed.). "Recent Works of Foster Associates." *Architecture and Urbanism* (February 1981).

Nakamura, Toshio (ed.). "Stansted Airport." *Architecture and Urbanism* (October 1991).

Nakamura, Toshio (ed.). "Works of Foster Associates." *Architecture and Urbanism* (September 1973).

"Norman Foster." *Monument Australia* (no. 6, 1995).

"Norman Foster." *Sunday Times Magazine* (6 October 1991).

"Norman Foster Profile." *Observer* (27 February 1983).

"Norman Foster: Royal Gold Medal Address." *Transactions 4 RIBA* (November 1983).

Padovan, Richard. "Urban Context: Hammersmith Centre." *International Architecture* (no. 1, 1979).

Pawley, Martin. "Norman Foster: Architecture's Local Boy Made Good." *Blueprint* (May 1984).

Pawley, Martin. "Renault Inspection." *Architects' Journal* (15 June 1983).

Pawley, Martin, Davies, Colin et al. "Hongkong and Shanghai Bank Special Issue." *Architectural Review* (April 1986).

Pidgeon, Monica (ed.). "Foster Associates' Recent Work." *Architectural Design* (May 1970).

Pidgeon, Monica (ed.). "Foster Associates' Recent Work." *Architectural Design* (November 1972).

Powell, Kenneth. "Architecture's Highest Flyer." *Building Design* (10 June 1994).

Powell, Kenneth. "Fosters Special: Current Buildings and Projects." *Architects' Journal* (27 July 1995).

Powell, Kenneth. "Modular Pupil." *RIBA Journal* (October 1993).

Puzey, Gordon. "Case Study: Down to Earth." *AJ Focus* (May 1991).

Rastorfer, Darl. "The Metal Skin in Technology of Foster Associates." *Architectural Record* (August 1985).

Safran, Yehuda. "Norman Foster: Le Carré d'Art Nîmes." *Domus* (July/August 1993).

Simon, Marlise. "Minimalism Clashes with Ancient Rome." *New York Times* (8 June 1993).

"Sir Norman Foster—Inaugural Academy Lecture." *Architectural Design* (November/December 1991).

Slessor, Catherine. "Office Politics." *Architects' Journal* (3 October 1990).

Spring, Martin. "Hi-Tech to Appropriate." *Architectural Design* (March 1976).

Stephens, Suzanne. "Modernism Reconstituted." *Progressive Architecture* (February 1979).

Sudjic, Deyan. "Re-inventing the Skyscraper." *Blueprint* (November 1985).

Sugimura, Kenji et al. "Hongkong Bank." *Architecture and Urbanism* (October 1983).

"Trois Usines en Angleterre." *Techniques et Architecture* (February/March 1974).

"Von hängenden Gärten ungläsernen Türmen." *Mensch & Büro* (February 1996).

Webb, Michael. "Portrait: Sir Norman Foster, England's Pre-eminent Architect Takes on Houses and Highrises." *Architectural Digest* (August 1995).

Welsh, John. "Art of Stone." *RIBA Journal* (January 1995).

Welsh, John. "Electric Blue." *RIBA Journal* (September 1996).

Williams, Stephanie. "Powerhouse." *Building Design* (3 February 1978).

Woodward, Christopher. "Ipswich Reflections." *Architectural Review* (September 1975).

Woojae, Lee (ed.). "Foster and Partners." *Korean Architects* (special issue, June 1995).

Collaborators

Otl Aicher

Arup Acoustics

Ove Arup & Partners

BAA Consultancy

Sandy Brown Associates

Richard Buckminster Fuller

Loren Butt

Cantor Seinuk

CAST SA

Cosentini

Richard Davies

Buro Happold

Davis Langdon and Everest

Desvigne and Dalnoky Paysagistes

Jolyon Drury Consultancy

Claude and Danielle Engle

Fisher Marantz Renfro Stone

Gardiner and Theobald

Gleeds

Halcrow Fox & Associates

Bill Hillier — Space Syntax Group

Anthony Hunt Associates Ltd

Jappsen & Stangier

Kaiser Bautechnik

Lerch Bates Associates

Derek Lovejoy Partnership

Rudi Meisel

Dr Meyer

Mott MacDonald

NACO

Northcroft Neighbour and Nicolson

Obayashi

Roger Preston and Partners

Quickborner Team

Schumann Smith

George Sexton Associates

Tim Smith Acoustics

Theatre Projects

Waterman Partnership

WET Design

WI Partnership

YRM Engineers Ltd

Acknowledgments

I would like to express my sincere thanks to the following people:

For contributing the text:
Alastair Best
Sir Norman Foster
Spencer de Grey
Katy Harris

For their tireless support:
Sir Norman Foster
Spencer de Grey
Katy Harris
Jo Olsen
Richard Burdett
Pamela Cronin
Jane Denholm
Sarah Wedderburn
the editorial team at The Images
Publishing Group

Photography credits:

Foster Asia: 153(6)

Xavier Basianas: 98 (11); 99 (13)

British Museum: 191 (3)

Richard Bryant: 69 (3, 4, 5, 7)

Martin Charles: 71 (2); 73 (7); 74 (14)

Peter Cook: 87 (8)

Richard Davies: 41 (6); 42 (7); 46 (7); 48 (12); 49 (14); 80 (1); 82 (1, 2); 83 (4); 89 (4); 90 (7, 8); 91 (11, 12); 92 (14); 93 (15, 16); 100 (2); 116 (6); 117 (8); 119 (10); 136 (3); 137 (5); 141 (3, 4, 5); 142 (7, 8); 147 (4); 160 (1); 161 (3, 4); 163 (3, 6); 164 (8); 165 (10); 166 (13); 167 (16); 173 (5, 6); 174 (8); 179 (12); 182 (2); 183 (3); 186 (1); 189 (8, 9); 192 (7); 193 (9); 194 (1); 204 (1); 205 (2); 215 (2); 216 (1, 2, 3); 217 (6, 7, 8); 218 (1); 230 (8) 213 (12)

J.C. Decaux: 62 (1, 2); 63 (4, 5)

Carlos Dominguez: 89 (4)

Patrick Drickey: 168 (1); 169 (5); 170 (9, 10); 171 (15, 16)

Richard Einzig: 20 (3, 4, 5, 6, 7); 23 (5)

Norman Foster: 42 (8)

Foster and Partners: 63 (3, 6); 138 (8, 9); 191 (5); 229 (3, 4)

Dennis Gilbert: 47 (9); 48 (10); 49 (13); 61 (17); 65 (3); 66 (5, 6); 67 (9, 10, 11); 86 (5); 87 (10); 102 (4, 5); 105 (4); 107 (10); 109 (3); 121 (4); 122 (6); 123 (7, 9); 125 (3); 126 (5); 127 (7, 8); 130 (13); 131 (15, 17); 134 (6, 7, 9, 10); 136 (3); 137 (5, 6)

Greg Girard: 154 (9)

Alastair Hunter: 43 (12)

Ben Johnson: 73 (8); 99 (15)

Ken Kirkwood: 22 (2, 3); 25 (3); 26 (4); 28 (2); 29 (5); 30 (10); 31 (11, 12); 45 (3); 46 (6); 229 (5)

Ian Lambot: 33 (2); 34 (5); 35 (6); 36 (7, 10); 37 (15, 16); 38 (18, 19); 72 (5, 6); 140 (2); 144 (11); 145 (2, 3); 228 (1, 2)

John Edward Linden: 96 (4); 99 (14); 129 (12)

Rudi Meisel: 166 (14, 15); 167 (17,18); 199 (6)

Tom Miller: 197 (3); 199 (7, 8); 206 (3, 4); 224 (1)

Mishima: 74 (13); 75 (15, 16); 77 (3); 79 (7, 8)

James H. Morris: 56 (2); 57 (4); 59 (13); 60 (14); 61 (15,16,18,19); 121 (5); 177 (3, 4); 178 (5, 6, 7); 179 (8); 180 (10, 11, 12)

Tim Street-Porter: 22 (1)

Paul Raftery: 133 (5); 135 (6)

Ken Shuttleworth: 215 (4)

Tim Soar: 57 (5)

Morley Von Sternberg: 184 (1, 2, 3)

Tecno Spa: 231 (10, 11)

Jens Willebrand: 105 (5); 108 (2); 212 (1); 213 (2, 3)

Jeremy Young: 210 (5, 6)

Nigel Young: 81 (3, 4, 5); 111 (5); 112 (6, 7, 8); 113 (9, 10, 11); 138 (7, 10); 200 (1); 201 (3); 209 (2, 3, 4); 211 (7); 220 (8); 229 (6)

Index

Bold page numbers refer to projects
included in Selected Works